THE FAB
BRITISH
ROCK'N'ROLL
INVASION OF 1964

PICTURE ACKNOWLEDGEMENTS

Aquarius: 50, 59, 142 (top) Barnaby's Picture Library: 11, 106, 121 (bottom)
Chappell Music Ltd/International Music Publications Ltd: 32, 41, 90 (top) EMI: 160, all pictures
Harry Goodwin: 74 (bottom), 76, 90 (bottom), 92 (left), 101 (top), 113 (bottom), 114 (bottom), 119, 131,
132, 155 (bottom) Ronald Grant Archives: 16 (bottom), 31, 37, 91 (top), 118 (bottom), 148 (left), 148 (right)
Hulton-Deutsch Collection: 13, 40-41, 45 (top), 67, 110 (top left), 140 (top), 141, 142 (bottom)
London Features International: 42, 43 (top), 66, 68 (right), 69, 70 (bottom), 149 Lumiere Picture Ltd: 101
(bottom) Magnum: 110-111, 151 Gered Mankowitz: 20, 28, 52, 75, 78 (top), 87, 92 (right), 98, 109, 130,
133 Melody Maker: 49 (bottom) Jan Oloffson: 8, 60 (bottom), 145 (right), 154 Pictorial Press: 5, 6, 10
(bottom), 14, 15, 23, 26, 29, 30, 35, 43 (bottom), 47 (bottom), 48 (top), 48 (left), 48 (bottom), 49 (top), 53
(bottom), 54, 55, 57 (top), 58, 65, 72, 73, 74 (top), 77, 78 (bottom), 79, 81, 82, 83, 84 (bottom), 85, 89, 93
(top), 94, 96, 97 (bottom), 100 (top), 100 (bottom), 105 (top), 105 (bottom), 107, 110 (bottom) (left), 110
(bottom) (right), 116 (bottom), 120 (bottom), 123, 126 (top), 126 (bottom), 127, 128, 135, 138, 141 (top),
144 (top), 146 (right), 152 (top), 155 (top), 156 (top), 156 (bottom), 157 Popperfoto: 9 (bottom), 10, 12
(top), 12 (bottom), 13, 16 (top), 18 (bottom), 21 (bottom), 25, 27, 30-31, 36, 40, 44, 47 (top), 51 (top), 53
(top), 60 (top), 63, 64, 68 (left), 70 (top), 88, 93 (bottom), 97 (top), 102, 112, 113 (top), 114 (top), 115, 116
(top), 118 (top), 120 (top), 121 (top), 124, 129, 134, 137, 139, 140, 141 (bottom), 143 (top), 143 (bottom),
144 (bottom), 145 (left), 146 (left), 147, 152 (bottom) Redferns: Bob Baker: 34 Gems: 7, 22, 39
David Redfern: 17, 24 (top), 24 (bottom), 33, 45 (bottom), 46, 56, 57 (bottom), 61, 84 (top), 91 (bottom),
95 (top), 99, 110 (bottom centre), 117, 122, 125, 140 (bottom) S & G: 71 Val Wilmer: 18 (top), 21 (top), 95
(bottom) Retna: Photofest: 64 (bottom); Michael Putland: 152-153 Topham: 19, 51 (bottom), 67
Warner Pathe: 150

Editor: MIKE EVANS
Design: ASHLEY WESTERN
Production Controller: MICHELLE THOMAS
Picture Research: CLAIRE TAYLOR

First published in 1994 by
Hamlyn, an imprint of
Reed Consumer Books Limited,
Michelin House, 81 Fulham Road,
London SW3 6RB
and Auckland, Melbourne, Singapore and Toronto

Library of Congress Cataloging-in-Publication Data

McAleer, Dave.
      The Fab British Rock'n'Roll Invasion of 1964 / Dave McAleer.
          p.   cm.
      ISBN 0-312-10191-0
      1. Rock music--United States--1961-1970--History and criticism.
      2. Rock music--Great Britain--1961-1970--History and criticism.
      I. Title. II. Title: Fab British Rock'n'Roll Invasion of 1964.
      III. Title: Fab British Rock'n'Roll Invasion of 1964.
    ML3534. M435 1994
    781.66'0941--dc20
                                                                                                          93-23583
                                                                                                                CIP
                                                                                                                MN

First Edition: March 1994
10 9 8 7 6 5 4 3 2 1

Produced by Mandarin Offset
Printed and bound in Hong Kong

THE FAB

BRITISH

ROCK'N'ROLL

INVASION OF 1964

DAVE McALEER

St. Martin's Press

New York

Contents

Foreword

I was greatly honoured to be asked to do the foreword for 'The Fab British Rock'n'Roll Invasion of 1964', which I think is a fabulous name for a fabulous book. Definitive in its writing, and highly informative for anyone that was not around in the 60's, the book is a comprehensive study of the music and bands from that period. Even the entry on Gerry and the Pacemakers made interesting reading for me because there was lots there I had forgotten. If I can forget it anyone can.

When the Pacemakers and I went to the States – which was very exciting as we had never been there before – we never realised the music would be accepted as it was, because we had started off playing American music by people like Chuck Berry and Fats Domino, and it was a great honour and privilege to be accepted by the American teenagers. We never thought that we would be doing the Ed Sullivan Show and suchlike, and so when we did we just couldn't believe it.

Reading the book through, it gives an insight to the bands around at that time, what they were doing and where they came from, the groups from London and elsewhere as well as the Manchester and Liverpool bands. And for me it's interesting to read about the bands from Liverpool who didn't make it, as well as those who did.

The other fascinating thing about this book is reading about the bands who I knew, lots of things about them that I didn't realise, and how hard they all had to work at it. Of course we thought at the time it was just fun and not really hard work at all. Reading through the book, it made me think 'Yeah, it was hard work but worth it' – the whole music scene was changed a great deal by the 'Beat Boom'.

I think it also changed all our lives from our youthful days. When we were in Liverpool and Hamburg, we were playing for a few quid because we enjoyed the music, and then we came to realise we could actually make a career out of it, out of something we loved, and actually get paid for it.

This was the life for us, and definitely for me. I thought that if I could continue in this business, entertaining people and songwriting and earning enough money to keep my family happy, that would do for me.

And thank goodness it's stayed that way. I'm very happy doing what I'm doing today. I'm still touring, we do Australia, the States, Canada, Singapore and Hong Kong, all over the world every year and we still enjoy it. Gerry and the Pacemakers are still rocking on.

A great book, I loved it! – and you are going to love it too, it's fabulous!

Take care and God bless.

Gerry Marsden

Introduction

Rock was unquestionably born in the USA. Yet this revolutionary music might well have died prematurely, if British groups had not breathed new life into it during the Beat Boom era.

The British have always loved rock. They idolised early rock'n'rollers such as Bill Haley, Elvis Presley, Jerry Lee Lewis, Gene Vincent and Buddy Holly. Britain was also not slow to find its own hit parade heroes, and the likes of Lonnie Donegan, Tommy Steele, Marty Wilde, Cliff Richard and Billy Fury scored hit after hit in the days when rock was young. In the early 1960s, the music softened on both sides of the Atlantic, and it was the British bands who rejuvenated rock and restored excitement and freshness to the music.

Anyone born in the last 35 years may find it difficult to imagine a world where British rock records and artists were considered essentially second-rate. However, this was the situation before The Beatles turned the pop music world upside down. They achieved the apparently impossible by leading a staggeringly successful British attack on the American charts in 1964, which buried once and for all the myth of British musical inferiority.

The intention of this book is to give a true picture of the Beat Boom years (warts and all), and to shed some light on areas and artists that may have been overlooked in previous accounts of this exciting era. Being British, I am very proud of the UK acts who emerged from rock's backwaters to rule the airwaves, and have a natural patriotic tendency to praise the efforts of my fellow countrymen. However, also being pro-originality and anti-imitation, my feeling is that credit is long overdue to many American recording artists and songwriters, who inspired the artists of the British Beat Boom in the first place, and penned many of their hits. I have, therefore, tried to look at this fascinating period in popular music history from an unbiased transatlantic viewpoint.

It may seem surprising that such a high percentage of Beat Boom hits were cover versions, or revivals of American records, and that most of the original recordings were made for the US R&B market. Many British artists simply watered down American R&B, aiming to make it more palatable and easily acceptable to white pop record buyers on both sides of the Atlantic. Even several of the group

The transatlantic connection was apparent from the start of the Beat Boom, with groups like the Beatles acknowledging American heroes like Gene Vincent (above)

The essence of Beat music was pure pop, as much to do with easy-on-the-ear acts like Peter and Gordon as the raunchier rock'n'rollers

names coined by British acts had already been used by American R&B combos. There is, therefore, a case for calling the decade the Stealing Sixties rather than the Swinging Sixties, and for suggesting that there might have been no Beat Boom or British Invasion without the input of black America - a fact that is equally true of rock'n'roll itself.

HIT PARADE HEROES

This book takes a close chronological look at the Beat Boom and the British Invasion, and includes every UK artist to debut on either the *NME* Top 30 (the chart most UK record buyers consulted at the time) or the American Top 100 singles charts of that era. It therefore includes not only the bands who bulldozed the barriers to the American chart, but also duos and solo performers such as Peter & Gordon, Tom Jones, Donovan, Dusty Springfield and Petula Clark. However, as successful as these other British artists were on the US singles chart between 1964-66, none emulated the groups by reaching the Top 10 of the American LP chart. For more background on the British acts who originally charted in the 1950s and early 1960s, the first book in this series, *Hit Parade Heroes*, should fit the bill.

It is a fact that if all the artists included were allocated the space they deserve, this book would be the size and price of an encyclopaedia. Since, quite understandably, this is impossible, the aim here is to make each artist's profile fact-packed but brief. Thus many oft-repeated stories have been omitted and several lesser known facts included. The book purposely avoids delving too deeply into the later careers of already well-documented giants of rock such as The Beatles and Rolling Stones, preferring instead to include many one-hit wonders, who also played essential, if smaller, roles in the Beat Boom saga. Since an artist's early days are usually the most interesting, the emphasis is generally placed on this period of their careers, and the majority of quotes are from their early press interviews. It's a fact of life that artists are nearly always more honest, candid and revealing when they feel somewhat insecure about their future and a still a little unsure of their talent. There is no doubt that fame does change an artist's viewpoint and that hindsight itself can be a hindrance to objectivity. It is also true that people often view the 'good old days' through rose coloured spectacles, the lenses of which tend to bend the truth.

FASHION AND TRENDS

This book glances at the transatlantic musical scene in the pre-Beat Boom period, and looks at the American artists who were hitting in their homeland between 1963-1967. There is also a chapter on the rock films produced in the era and British television and radio in the mid 1960s, as well as a brief examination of the British social scene and the UK's fashions and trends of the time. In addition, the more pop-trivia minded will find there is no shortage of charts, lists and interesting – and often little known – facts.

It would be wonderful to say that all the genuinely original, unique and most talented British artists of the period were successful and are therefore included.

Fun was usually the theme with groups like Freddie & The Dreamers (left) while the Mersey pals pose with Billy J., Cilla and Gerry, with attendant Pacemakers and Dakotas

It would also be great to affirm that no over-hyped minor talents are present. Sadly, the very nature of the record industry dictates that neither fact could be true for the Beat Boom era, nor indeed any other period before or since. Also, when reading this book, it is worth bearing in mind that musical trends always overlap - they never occur isolated in a cultural vacuum; at the same time that the Beat Boom grew in importance, peaked and faded, other musical styles also enjoyed varying degrees of success on both sides of the Atlantic Ocean.

If anything has been learned from my 30 years in the music business or 40 years as a record and trivia collector, it is that every record and recording artist has an interesting story, and that there are always at least a handful of people who know more about a particular act or record than anyone else. Thankfully, every performer, no matter how small on the hit scale, has solid died-in-the-wool fans who are often only too happy to put pen to paper and share some of their knowledge - thus adding more fascinating facts to the story of popular music. If you are one of these experts, please don't hesitate to send me your comments via the publishers of this book.

THANKS

I would like to take this opportunity of thanking Derek Brecknock, Gerry Marsden, the McAleer clan, Jon Philibert, and the many performers, producers and back room boys who have shared their often amazing stories with me over the years. I would also like to praise the work of the record papers of the period and the many authors of previous books covering this exciting era.

Also a very special thank you goes to Mike Evans, Billie Gordon and John Tobler for all their work on this project.

Beat before the boom

PRE-SIXTIES POP

It may come as a surprise to some, but British beat music was not born in a Liverpool cellar at the turn of the 1960s. It had been positively thriving since 1956, when Lonnie Donegan took a ride on the 'Rock Island Line', and teenager Tommy Steele exploded on to the UK scene with the primitive self-penned 'Rock With The Caveman'.

The original British Beat music boomed in 1957. First of all there was an unprecedented interest in skiffle, a do-it-yourself jug band styled music that combined folk and rock, which Lonnie Donegan so successfully introduced the previous year. Forming a skiffle group needed little financial outlay, and musical ability was not high on the list of requirements for would-be skifflers. If you could pick up a cheap guitar, purloin a washboard and thimbles, or procure a tea-chest, broom handle and length of string (for a make-shift double bass), you were set to strum, scrape or plunk your way to fame and fortune. Literally thousands of skiffle groups sprung up all around Britain and it seemed as if every teenager in the UK was in one. The repertoire of most of these home-grown bands included current skiffle and rock'n'roll hits mixed with American folk or blues songs (often from the catalogues of early working-class heroes Woody Guthrie and Leadbelly). Few people, if

Poles apart; early UK forays into the American charts included the seminal skiffle of Lonnie Donegan (above) and the lush string sounds of Mantovani and his Orchestra

any, predicted the meteoric rise of the music, and fewer still foresaw how soon the bubble would burst. Even before many Donegan-wanna-bes had paid off the first instalments on their guitars, skiffle was on the slide, and a multitude of non-musical musicians had to abandon their washboards and turn in their tea-chests. Although this craze was only short-lived, it encouraged thousands of young Britons to pick up instruments for the first time, and many of these amateur skifflers went on to become international rock heroes in the 1960s.

As skiffle was making its spectacular entrance and exit, rock'n'roll was growing in stature at an ever-increasing pace. Most American rock heroes hit equally hard in Britain. Bill Haley & The Comets, who at one time had five singles simultaneously in the UK Top 20, kept Britain's rock'n'roll throne warm until Elvis Presley came bopping along to claim it as his own as undisputed King. The British teenage public treated rock icons such as Gene Vincent, Jerry Lee Lewis, Little Richard, Buddy Holly and Eddie Cochran like gods. Their records and – in some cases – stage shows, were closely studied not only by Britain's fast-growing rock'n'roll fraternity, but also by countless would-be rock stars of the future around the British Isles.

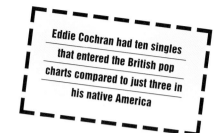

Eddie Cochran had ten singles that entered the British pop charts compared to just three in his native America

MOVE IT

In those first years after 'Rock Around The Clock' shook up the record market, many British popular song-writers had trouble mastering the new musical medium. This meant that UK rockers like Tommy Steele, Terry Dene and Marty Wilde often had to resort to covering American songs to stand any chance of hitting in their homeland. Then, in the autumn of 1958, 'Move It', a single penned by one of his group members, Ian Samwell, gave Cliff Richard a major UK hit with his first release. This outstanding record sent out an early warning to the world - that Britain could write and sing rock as well as the Americans.

In 1959, while Liverpool-born Billy Fury and Londoner Johnny Kidd actually released self-composed rock records on a par with many Americans, Britain's MOR merchants were having a bumper year in the USA. Orchestra leader Mantovani placed five albums simultaneously in the stereo chart (there were separate lists in those days for mono and stereo LPs), and at one time the big bands of Reg Owen and Cyril Stapleton were alongside Chris Barber's Jazz Band in the US Top 20 singles. It was Barber who helped launch the British traditional jazz (trad) craze that swept Britain at the turn of the decade.

Trad, which had been born in the jazz clubs of New Orleans and Chicago in the 1920s, had been building a British following since the end of World War II. It was the musical style that superseded skiffle in the cellar clubs, and by 1961, it had worked its way overground to become as successful on record as skiffle, even

Tommy Steele was the first in a long line of British rock'n'roll stars whose stated ambition was to become an 'all-round entertainer'

The Springfields (right) were an
early example of a Sixties vocal
group edging into territory that
until then had been dominated by
solo singers like Cliff Richard

though it attracted less would-be performers. The music's best known exponents
were the bands of Kenny Ball, Chris Barber and Acker Bilk, all of whom had some
American success. Trad managed to survive the arrival in Britain of The Twist in
1962, but sank alongside Chubby Checker's flagship at about the same time as The
Beatles first appeared on the scene.

POLITE POP

Rock on both sides of the Atlantic Ocean certainly softened in the early 1960s. But
the new decade also saw the end of Britain's almost total reliance on American
songs and production ideas. Many British artists were now recording original
home-grown material, and several of their singles boasted clever ear-catching
arrangements and fresh commercial production ideas. Among the more interesting
and inventive British artists of that era were teen idol Adam Faith, 14-year-old
Helen Shapiro, John Leyton, folk singer Karl Denver and actor turned singer/song-
writer Anthony Newley. Also deserving of praise were Eden Kane and Joe Brown
who, recorded 'I'm Henry The Eighth I Am' four years before Herman's Hermits
took it to the top of the US chart. Included among the pop back room boys of

whom Britain could be justly proud at the time were producers Joe Meek, Tony Hatch, Norrie Paramor and George Martin, and songwriters Jerry Lordan, Lionel Bart and Johnny Worth.

When 1962 dawned, the only piece missing from the British music jigsaw was original vocal groups. There were the clean-cut King Brothers, The Mudlarks and The Avons, whose only successes had been with cover versions, and Everly Brothers clones like The Allisons and The Brook Brothers. The only group who appeared to have that extra 'something' were The Springfields (including future solo star Dusty Springfield). Britain, nevertheless, had several first division instrumental combos, the most popular and influential being Cliff Richard's backing band The Shadows. It's astounding that this group, who have had a British chart span of over 30 years, have yet to crack the US Top 100, although a cover version of their first British No. 1 'Apache', sold over a million Stateside for Danish guitarist Jorgen Ingmann. The only British group to really make their mark in America in the pre-Beat Boom era were Billy Fury's backing band The Tornados, whose single 'Telstar' topped the US chart in late 1962, as The Beatles were starting to attract attention in the UK.

'Mr' Acker Bilk, usually with the bowler hat and striped waistcoat, was at the commercial sharp end of the short-lived trad jazz boom

Britannia waives the rules

EARLY UK HITS IN THE US

Ballad singer Matt Monro was hailed by critics as a Britain's answer to Frank Sinatra

Apart from being the world's largest record buying market and the home of rock, America was also the country that set most musical trends around the globe. It was, therefore, the dream of every British artist in those pre-Beat Boom years to break into the American chart, albeit in the lower reaches of the Top 100.

Although few people outside the music industry were aware of it, the first American chart appeared in 1890. In its first forty years, this barometer of American public taste often included recordings by British-born artists and in fact in that era, Irish born George J. Gaskin amassed more No. 1s than The Beatles ever managed, and British vocalists like John McCormack, tartan-wearing Sir Harry Lauder and Lancashire lassie Ada Jones regularly reached the best sellers.

In the 1930s and 1940s, bands like those of Ray Noble, Ambrose and Joe Loss had some US successes, as did British songbirds Gracie Fields and Anne Shelton. The first half of the 1950s found British bands and orchestras continuing to make their presence felt, with Top 20 entries by Mantovani, Frank Chacksfield, Edmundo Ros and Frank Weir. The 'man with the golden trumpet', Eddie Calvert, also reached the Top 10, as did balladeer David Whitfield and the 'Forces Sweetheart', Vera Lynn, who spent nine weeks at the top with 'Auf Wiederseh'n Sweetheart'.

When rock'n'roll rocked pop music's foundations there was less demand for the high class middle-of-the-road recordings that Britain specialised in, and the appearance of a UK act in the US Top 10 in the late 1950s was a rarity. Lonnie Donegan's 'Rock Island Line' made the excursion as early as 1956, and 'Rainbow', the B-side of Russ Hamilton's British hit 'We Will Make Love', found a pot of gold in 1957 (a year when only four UK recordings made the Top 100). There was a similarly poor showing in 1958, when only young Laurie London kept the Union Jack flying with his chart topping revival of a gospel standard, 'He's Got The Whole World (In His Hands)'. Transatlantic hits by British artists were so rare that the UK music media handed out plaudits to any UK produced record that even managed to creep into the bottom end of the US Top 100. One such single was an instrumental stomper, 'Fried Onions', recorded by Lord Rockingham's XI. It may have only reached No. 96, but it proved British acts could make it Stateside with originals.

STRANGERS ON THE SHORE

In 1959, for the first time in modern recording history, three British singles stood simultaneously in the US Top 20, and all were instrumentals. They were Reg Owen's infectious 'Manhattan Spiritual', the Chris Barber Jazz Band's 'Petite Fleur' (which featured clarinet player Monty Sunshine) and the Cyril Stapleton Orchestra's 'The Children's Marching Song' ('Nick Nack Paddy Wack'). That year also saw

British-based Australian singer Frank Ifield (left) with dance band leader Joe Loss

the first vocal British rock record crack the US Top 40, Cliff Richard's UK No. 1 'Living Doll', which outpaced a couple of covers. Marty Wilde was the next UK rocker to find a modicum of fame across the Atlantic, when his self-composed 'Bad Boy' briefly visited the top half of the Top 100, even though there were several American versions on the market. A cover war also raged over the song 'Look For A Star', with London teenager Garry Mills coming second in a four-horse chart race to the similarly named Garry Miles - a nom-de-disque chosen especially for this record by singer/songwriter Buzz Cason!

America opened up a little more to British talent in 1961. Fourteen-year-old film star Hayley Mills (no relation to Garry) took the novelty 'Let's Get Together' into the Top 10 and balladeer Matt Monro made the Top 20 with 'My Kind Of Girl'. It was also record breaking time for Lonnie Donegan, who became the only British artist in the pre-Beatles era to clock up two Top 10 hits. He completed his double with a timely reissue of his 1959 UK hit 'Does Your Chewing Gum Lose Its Flavour (On The Bedpost Overnight)', a novelty number that Donegan discovered in a 25-year-old Boy Scouts song-book. Britain's 'Kings Of Trad', Acker Bilk and Kenny Ball both had Top 3 singles in 1962 with the haunting 'Stranger On The Shore' and the bouncy 'Midnight In Moscow' respectively. However, this did not herald the launch of a trad boom in the USA - in fact, many Americans did not realise they were buying records by jazz acts. In reality, 1962 was a boom year for

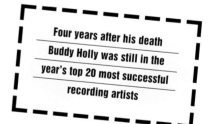

Four years after his death Buddy Holly was still in the year's top 20 most successful recording artists

British singles. The Tornados topped the chart with their five million selling 'Telstar', an instrumental tribute to the communications satellite that linked Europe and America, while Frank Ifield's revival of 'I Remember You' and 'Silver Threads And Golden Needles' by The Springfields both reached the Top 20.

In 1963, the year when Britain enjoyed its first taste of the Beat Boom, America ignored all the new groups the old country offered them. Cliff Richard had his most successful US year thus far, charting with 'Lucky Lips' and 'It's All In The Game'. The only single by a new UK act that Americans bought in any quantity was by female duo The Caravelles, whose updating of 'You Don't Have To Be A Baby To Cry' reached the Top 3 a couple of weeks before the release of The Beatles' fifth British hit single, 'I Want To Hold Your Hand'......

Cutsie transatlantic charters the Caravelles consisted of Andrea Simpson (left) and Lois Wilkinson. (below), The Tornados took 'Telstar' into the pop stratosphere

A shot of rhythm and blues

FROM CHICAGO TO LONDON

The American music trade paper *Billboard* first coined the term Rhythm & Blues (R&B) in 1948, as a catch-all phrase to describe the whole spectrum of popular music played by African Americans. By the mid-1950s, one tributary of this rich R&B river merged with country & western (C&W) and mainstream pop to form rock'n'roll. Simultaneously, other streams, including all the varied forms of blues, continued to flow along uninterrupted. Rock-oriented R&B singers like Chuck Berry, Little Richard and Fats Domino became multi-racial favourites as rock'n'roll took over the pop and R&B airwaves, while artists whose style veered more towards the blues end of R&B were left relatively high and dry in their homeland.

British blues boom pioneers Cyril 'Squirrel' Davies (left) on harp, and guitarist/vocalist Alexis Korner

In late 1950s Britain, not only did R&B rockers sell well, but there was also growing interest in less obviously commercial R&B performers, whose songs were incorporated into the acts of several UK jazz and skiffle groups. In 1961, two skiffle and traditional jazz veterans, guitarist Alexis Korner and harmonica man Cyril Davies, formed Blues Inc., who are regarded as Britain's first R&B group. They were basically a R&B-revivalist band, whose style owed more to the blues, jazz and folk roots of the music than to contemporary American R&B. The group's music

was not overly influential, but their gigs became a gathering place for would-be rhythm and blues musicians, and a list of those who played with Blues Inc. reads like a 'Who's-Who' of 1960s UK Rock. Notable participants included Mick Jagger, Charlie Watts and Brian Jones (Rolling Stones), Ginger Baker and Jack Bruce (Cream), Paul Jones (Manfred Mann) and John Mayall. Later in life, Korner, who was literally the corner-stone of British R&B, was instrumental in the formation of both Free and Led Zeppelin.

CULT MUSIC

Among the other early R&B acts in Britain were singer/pianist Georgie Fame & The Blue Flames, John Mayall & Blues Syndicate from Manchester and the London based Mann-Hugg Blues Brothers (who evolved into Manfred Mann). The music of these groups was also styled on the less-commercial jazz and blues end of R&B – for British R&B to grow, it needed more commercially minded performers.

Contemporary commercial R&B had not gone unnoticed in Britain. Occasionally a record from this specialised genre would crossover into the UK pop chart, but as a rule, it was too uninhibited to get mass acceptance. The music, nonetheless, had attracted a growing number of fans since the late 1950s, the period when rock'n'roll softened up and lost its teeth. In their quest for real excitement on

Georgie Fame (above) was initially based in London's Flamingo Club, while John Mayall (right, with his family) worked from Manchester

record, many people turned to R&B, and singles such as the anthemic two part classic 'What I'd Say' by Ray Charles and 'Shout' by The Isley Brothers, more than fulfilled their needs. By the start of the 1960s, hundreds of record buyers were actively seeking out the latest US R&B sounds. There was a growing demand for product by people like Bobby Bland, James Brown, The Miracles, Solomon Burke and Ike & Tina Turner. It was a time of great change, and many of the R&B

The early 'Stones, with (left to right)
Bill Wyman, Brian Jones, Charlie
Watts, Mick Jagger and a youthful
looking Keith Richards

records released then helped shape the music of the 1960s. Among those ground-breaking singles were Barrett Strong's original version of 'Money', Jessie Hill's call and response classic 'Ooh Poo Pah Doo' and 'I Found A Love' by The Falcons (featuring Wilson Pickett), the last often being credited with starting soul music as we know it. Many newly-converted R&B fans also attempted to catch up with records they had missed in the early rock days. Delving back, some discovered the delights of doo-wop (which was making a US comeback in 1960) whilst others, impressed by newer releases from acts like Hank Ballard & The Midnighters, Little Willie John and James Brown, checked out their back catalogues. Many more fans dug deep into the vaults of R&B rockers like Chuck Berry and Bo Diddley, and contemporary blues-based legends such as Muddy Waters, Jimmy Reed, Howlin' Wolf and Slim Harpo.

Mick Jagger and Brian Jones were big fans of commercial American R&B of the mid-to-late-1950s. Together with Jagger's old school friend and fellow fanatic Keith Richards, they decided to form a group to perform songs by their favourite US artists. They named it after a Muddy Waters composition, 'Rollin' Stone', and made their stage debut on 'R&B Night' at the Marquee in London's Oxford Street in July 1962.

> *"We do not use any original material – after all, can you imagine a British composed R&B number – it just wouldn't make it"*
> *Mick Jagger, Jazz News*

CAN'T JUDGE A BOOK

On the day The Beatles' R&B-influenced debut single, 'Love Me Do', entered the Top 30, The Rolling Stones recorded their first demo session, at which they borrowed freely from their mentors. The songs they chose were a cover of Bo Diddley's then current single, 'You Can't Judge A Book', Jimmy Reed's hypnotic 1961 US-only release 'Close Together', and 'Soon Forgotten', a track from the LP Muddy Waters At Newport. All three tracks were by acts who US R&B audiences considered to be past their prime.

In their first press write-up, *Record Mirror* noted 'The Rolling Stones are probably destined to be the biggest group on the R&B scene, if it continues to flourish.'

It continued 'they have achieved the American sound better than any other group in Britain', pointing out that 'unlike all the other British R&B groups, The Rolling Stones have a definite visual appeal. They aren't jazzmen who were doing trad. They are genuine R&B fanatics, and they sing and play in a way that one would expect more from a coloured American R&B team than a bunch of white boys.' The Stones themselves dismissed the possibility of writing their own material, proudly stating, 'We do not use any original material – after all, can you imagine a British composed R&B number – it just wouldn't make it..'

While London was becoming a hotbed for new R&B performers, the music scenes in Liverpool, Manchester, and indeed Hamburg also had their share of artists incorporating commercial R&B material into their acts. Apart from The Beatles, Merseyside groups like The Big Three, Kingsize Taylor & The Dominoes (not to be confused with the US R&B group), The Searchers and Howie Casey & The Seniors more than merit a mention in any discussion on the early days of British rhythm and blues.

On the UK record front in 1962, influential television and record producer Jack Good was responsible for two mould-shattering British R&B releases, Jimmy Powell's much-underrated raver 'Sugar Babe' (first recorded by New Orleans singer Buster Brown), and later in the year Alexis Korner's album, R&B From The Marquee. Powell, incidentally, was billed in the all-star film, *It's Trad, Dad!*, but if you blinked, you would have missed him. Other outstanding UK R&B oriented singles by British artists that year included gems from Chris Farlowe and Jackie Lynton. Farlowe released an independently produced version of Ray (Swayne) & Bob (Appleberry)'s 'Air Travel', and distinctive high-voiced Lynton's followed his underrated 'Over The Rainbow' with a unusually interesting interpretation of another oldie 'All Of Me'.

Despite a chart-topping single with 'Out Of Time' in 1966, Chris Farlow remained something of a 'singer's singer' on the R&B scene

WHITE BOYS BLUES

By the time The Beatles first charted with 'Love Me Do' in October 1962, the UK R&B movement was already gaining momentum, and was soon catapulted from cult to full commercial status. By spring 1963 it had become the most talked about music form on the British pop scene, as R&B clubs sprouted up all over the country. Many of the early British R&B-oriented acts genuinely had a great affection for the music they were playing. However, once the R&B bandwagon starting rolling, other groups, who saw the music more as a meal ticket, clambered aboard by adding US R&B material, both ancient and modern, to their repertoires. R&B soon became the most quoted and least understood musical term of the early 1960s, with countless UK pop groups claiming to be R&B combos. Controversy raged in the music press over what constituted a R&B record or act, and many fans of the music dismissed the whole British movement as simply 'pale imitations' of the real thing (it was these purists who formed the core of fans for the American soul music craze that was to follow). To most of the British record buying public in 1963, however, R&B was the sound created by The Beatles and other Beat Boom groups; and they could not get enough of it. Fifteen years after the term was coined to describe the music of black America, rhythm and blues had become synonymous with white British beat music.

Birth of the beat boom

1963 – THE LIVERPOOL SOUND

1962 was a good year for British acts in the UK. Between them, Cliff Richard, The Shadows and Frank Ifield held the No. 1 position for 28 weeks. In actuality only Elvis Presley (who was the year's most successful chart act), Chubby Checker, Ray Charles, and one-hit wonders B. Bumble & The Stingers managed to wave the Stars and Stripes in the top slot during that twelve-month period.

Hopes were high in the British music industry that UK acts could repeat that feat the following year, but no one anticipated just how successful they would be. 1963 opened with the lively instrumental 'Dance On' by The Shadows, replacing their lead singer Cliff Richard's 'The Next Time', at the top of the singles chart. It looked as though it would be the year of the British instrumental when 'Diamonds', recorded by ex-Shadows, Jet Harris & Tony Meehan, overtook their old group at the summit. This Jerry Lordan composed gem fought off all-comers for four weeks and at one time headed an unprecedented all instrumental Top 3. Another record breaking feat followed in late February, when British born and Australian bred Frank Ifield claimed his third consecutive chart topper with a revival of Gogi Grant's 1956 US No. 1, 'Wayward Wind'. As stunning as these events were, the British record buying public were far more interested in the rapid rise of 'Please Please Me', the second single by Liverpool group The Beatles, which shared the top spot with Ifield's record.

When the year started, relatively few people outside Liverpool had heard of The Beatles, and fewer still knew about the abundance of groups in the Merseyside area – both these situations were quickly rectified. On February 2, 'Please Please Me' entered the Top 30 at No. 17, and in three weeks it was No. 1. One month later, another Liverpool band, Gerry & The Pacemakers also debuted at 17. Their single,

The Beatles, seen (below left) with Epstein stable-mates (left to right) Gerry and The Pacemakers, Epstein himself, and Billy J.Kramer (third from right) with The Dakotas

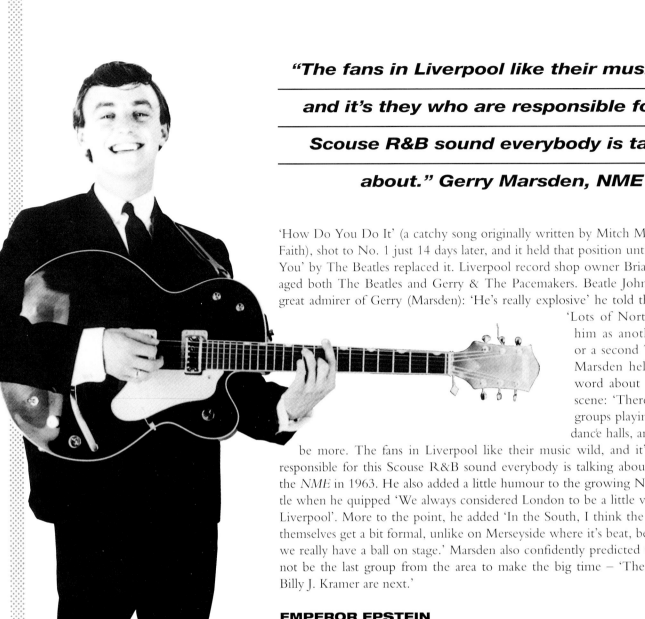

> **"The fans in Liverpool like their music wild, and it's they who are responsible for this Scouse R&B sound everybody is talking about." Gerry Marsden, NME**

'How Do You Do It' (a catchy song originally written by Mitch Murray for Adam Faith), shot to No. 1 just 14 days later, and it held that position until 'From Me To You' by The Beatles replaced it. Liverpool record shop owner Brian Epstein managed both The Beatles and Gerry & The Pacemakers. Beatle John Lennon was a great admirer of Gerry (Marsden): 'He's really explosive' he told the press, adding 'Lots of Northern girls class him as another Joe Brown or a second Tommy Steele'. Marsden helped spread the word about the Merseybeat scene: 'There are about 170 groups playing the clubs and dance halls, and there used to be more. The fans in Liverpool like their music wild, and it's they who are responsible for this Scouse R&B sound everybody is talking about' Marsden told the *NME* in 1963. He also added a little humour to the growing North-South battle when he quipped 'We always considered London to be a little village outside of Liverpool'. More to the point, he added 'In the South, I think the groups have let themselves get a bit formal, unlike on Merseyside where it's beat, beat all the way – we really have a ball on stage.' Marsden also confidently predicted that they would not be the last group from the area to make the big time – 'The Big Three and Billy J. Kramer are next.'

EMPEROR EPSTEIN

To many people's astonishment The Big Three never achieved the expected breakthrough. They only managed a minor hit with the Mitch Murray composition 'By The Way'. Kramer, on the other hand, was one of the year's major success stories. The vocalist, who bore a passing resemblance to another local pop hero Billy Fury, started with Liverpool combo The Coasters (no connection with the top selling US R&B team). When Brian Epstein took him under his wing in early 1963, the noted manager recruited Manchester group The Dakotas to back him. Kramer's debut release was the John Lennon & Paul McCartney song 'Do You Want To Know A Secret', a catchy pop pearl that pushed its composers' group, The Beatles, out of the top spot. Kramer's success came as no surprise to Lennon & McCartney, who had earlier commented 'So far as the British scene is concerned, we believe that Billy will take over from where Elvis Presley is beginning to leave off.' George Martin, Kramer's producer (and often keyboard player on record), added 'I'm certain Billy has more than sufficient singing talent, good looks and personality to become one of the most important new hit parade stars of 1963.' Martin also expressed the opinion that 'instrumentally The Dakotas are probably better than The Beatles and The Pacemakers.' Incidentally, Kramer, whose November 1963 Stateside promotional trip made him the very first of the British Beat Boom acts to visit the US, actually described his music as 'Liverpool Blues'. This he explained 'is

Noted for their instrumental prowess, The Dakotas did a 'Shadows' with a hit without their name vocalist Billy J. Kramer

a variation of R&B, which is different from US R&B, but as far as I'm concerned, that doesn't make it less authentic.' He emphasised 'Liverpool R&B is different, just listen to the records that come from there – but it is rhythm and blues. I am in the same field of music as Muddy Waters and Howlin' Wolf, only our kind of R&B is more commercial.'

There seemed no place at the top for anyone but acts from Epstein's burgeoning stable, and it came as no surprise when Gerry & The Pacemakers' 'I Like It' took over from Kramer. This latter success stretched Epstein's consecutive span

> ## "Instrumentally The Dakotas are probably better than The Beatles and The Pacemakers."
> ### George Martin

at the summit to 14 weeks, and in doing so it stopped The Shadows scoring their third successive No. 1 with 'Atlantis'. Record sales were rocketing in Britain, and in the five months since 'Please Please Me', Epstein's acts alone sold an unprecedented 2.5 million singles in the UK.

MERSEY MANIA

By June, every British pop record buyer was talking about the 'Liverpool Sound', a tag which threw together all the acts from the Merseyside area. George Martin, the producer of the three chart-topping Scouse super groups, was adamant there was no such thing. 'I prefer to talk of a Beatles sound,' he explained, 'after all they got the whole thing started,' adding 'not that the other groups copy them. Quite the contrary, for their styles are totally different.' One thing there was no doubt about – the Beat Boom was well under way. When asked why he thought the Beat Boom had happened, John Lennon said 'The beat has always been there and nobody has ever tired of it. However, just lately it's become available on disc again and this has triggered it all off'. He added 'America has some really great groups that we never hear in Britain, probably because they're too bluesy, too – as they say – uncommercial. Which is exactly what we were called at one time.'

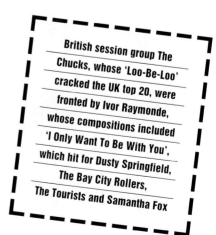

British session group The Chucks, whose 'Loo-Be-Loo' cracked the UK top 20, were fronted by Ivor Raymonde, whose compositions included 'I Only Want To Be With You', which hit for Dusty Springfield, The Bay City Rollers, The Tourists and Samantha Fox

Freddie & The Dreamers (right) were hardly pop pin-ups, but The Merseybeats (below) were greeted with hysteria across the country

"We've always been daft, I mean you couldn't call me a sex idol, could you? Collectively we're no glamour boys."

Freddie Garrity

Most early Beat Boom acts featured a good proportion of US R&B songs in their repertoires, and it was not long before British bands were regularly raiding American R&B catalogues as a source of material to record. The first group to score with a revival of a R&B number in the Beat Boom were Freddie & The Dreamers, whose anglicised treatment of James Ray's US hit, 'If You Gotta Make A Fool Of Somebody', narrowly missed the top. Incidentally, it had been that song, rather than the singers, that initially interested their producer John Burgess at Columbia Records, when John Barry originally played him a demo of Freddie & The Dreamers. The group came under fire from R&B fans for this recording. Freddie Garrity was not slow to say, 'To be honest, I think the original version is better than ours, but I'm not complaining that we got the hit and he didn't.' Interestingly, the first soloist to chart with a R&B revival hit in 1963 was Buddy Holly. The late singer not only scored with Chuck Berry's 'Brown-Eyed Handsome Man' but also with a revival of 'Bo Diddley', an earlier R&B hit for Diddley himself. Ex-milkman Freddie and the rest of his Manchester-based band were unique; their records were on a par with any of the UK bands of the era, and their humorous stage act had no equal. They did not just move on stage, they cavorted about in an outlandish fashion, the like of which the public had not seen before, or indeed since. The Shadows and their 'Shadows Walk' had set the standard for British group performances, and Freddie & The Dreamers showed the extremes that choreographed stage movements could go to. 'We've always been daft' Garrity admitted, adding 'I mean you couldn't call me a sex-idol, could you? Collectively, we're no glamour boys.' They followed their debut hit with 'I'm Telling You Now', which went on to top the US chart in 1965. Five months after opening their chart account, the zany group completed their hat trick of Top 3 UK singles with 'You Were Made For Me'.

NORTHERN LIGHTS

There was a new excitement in the air. There had been no shortage of hit parade heroes in Britain before, but these new groups cleaned away the cobwebs that had formed on the UK music scene. Suddenly Britain's rock recording artists had a niche of their own – they were no longer simply mirror images of their American counterparts. There were still more than enough US clones on the British scene, but for the first time many acts were self-sufficient, and several were extremely creative and indeed innovative. If one had to say briefly what the most striking difference was between the 1963 British pop groups and the vast majority of earlier UK rock-orientated artists, the most obvious answer would have to be their marked regional accents. It was no longer essential for the lead singer to sound as if he had been born in the USA, or, at the very least, on an island in the mid-Atlantic. Suddenly there were singers whose voices instantly betrayed their North-of-England origins. Northern accents, which people had for so long associated with lovable, if sometimes gormless, music hall characters like George Formby and Gracie Fields, reappeared on the entertainment scene in a new light and helped change British popular music forever.

Brian Poole and The Tremeloes were the first Southerners in the Beat Boom chart stakes

Something you can't accuse the record business of is being slow to move when a new musical trend becomes obvious. Groups from Merseyside to Manchester were suddenly 'in', and armies of A&R men boarded the north-bound bandwagon, rushing to Scouseland with briefcases crammed with contracts. The pop media quickly climbed aboard too, and Northern Beat columns became regular features in most of the record papers.

One of the first A&R men to hotfoot it to the North was John Schroeder of Oriole Records (the producer/writer who had played a major role in Helen Shapiro's career). 'I want to capture the authentic Liverpool Beat sound' Schroeder said. He recorded 15 groups including the much-heralded Faron's Flamingos, Earl

The Searchers featured (left to right) Chris Curtis, John McNally, Mike Pender and Tony Jackson

Preston & The TTs, The Mersey Beats, Ian & The Zodiacs and Derry Wilkie & The Pressmen. Schroeder finished the double album in the time it takes nowadays to record a single. It reached the Top 20, but none of the singles taken from the album, This Is Merseybeat, charted. They simply got lost among the scores of other group records released by an industry desperate to get their piece of the pop pie.

> *"They do not have good enough stage acts to match up to their hit discs"*
> *Brian Poole on Mersey bands*

GOIN' SEARCHIN'
It may have been the start of a new era for British artists, but there was still a dearth of great British songs for them to record. Therefore, in the time-honoured UK fashion, many of the acts who could not convince Lennon & McCartney to pen a song for them turned to America for material to record. Included among these was the first band from the South to benefit from the group explosion, Brian Poole & The Tremeloes, who first hit the heights with an update of 'Twist & Shout'. American artists the Top Notes, Carla Thomas and The Isley Brothers had previously recorded the song, but it was probably The Beatles interpretation that the group were most familiar with. Poole admitted to borrowing from The Beatles treatment, 'You've only got to hear the two versions to spot the resemblance' he conceded. Before the year was out, Poole & The Tremeloes were topping the chart with their diluted delivery of 'Do You Love Me', a song which had given The Contours a US Top 3 hit and had introduced the Dave Clark Five to the UK Top 30. Poole was not unduly worried about the competition from Clark but said, 'What might worry us is if they started re-plugging the fabulous Contours original.' Poole, whose group's image owed as much to The Shadows as The Beatles, summed up the their music by saying 'our policy is this: as musical tastes change, we'll change.' Like so many others in 1963, the group purported to be a R&B act, saying 'We find that audiences really go for the big beat, US Negro style'. The Tremeloes always prided themselves on their live shows, and when

asked about the Liverpool groups, Poole was a little scathing, commenting 'They do not have good enough stage acts to match up to their hit discs.'

The hugely successful pop TV series *Thank Your Lucky Stars* celebrated its 100th edition in August 1963. Among the stars on that show were The Tremeloes and Liverpool quartet The Searchers, who like their southern contemporaries first scored with a cover of an early sixties R&B hit. In early 1963, The Searchers had recorded their own album (which cost them the princely sum of £40) and sent it to producer/songwriter Tony Hatch at Pye Records. Hatch quickly realised they were the group he had been searching for. For their first single he re-recorded a track from their LP, 'Sweets For My Sweet', which shot to the top in the UK. The record so impressed John Lennon that at the time he called it 'The best disc ever from a Liverpool group.' Incidentally, despite this accolade, The Searchers declined to work out of the Merseyside area until the record was safely situated in the Top 10. The media were quick to point out The Searchers sounded different from other Liverpool groups. Bass guitarist Tony Jackson's falsetto gave them more of an American sound, which even resulted in their being compared with the Four Seasons. As was the case with most UK groups of the period, The Searchers' repertoire contained many US R&B songs, but they wisely refused to call themselves a R&B band. When asked how the Liverpool sound had come about, drummer Chris Curtis explained 'When the big beat cooled off in the rest of the country, it stayed tops in Liverpool. This meant the groups went on singing and playing it.' Amidst all the furore about Merseyside bands, Jackson added a warning note, 'The majority of Liverpool's most popular groups have already signed to recording contracts, and the area is pretty well milked. It will take some years before a new crop of groups with individual styles develop.'

The Fourmost, another of the foremost bands in Liverpool, were fortunate enough to have their first two singles penned by Lennon & McCartney. At the same time that the quirky quartet were forging their first hit, 'Hello Little Girl' (a composition that Gerry & The Pacemakers seriously considered as a second single),

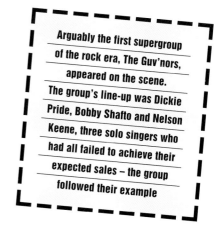

Arguably the first supergroup of the rock era, The Guv'nors, appeared on the scene. The group's line-up was Dickie Pride, Bobby Shafto and Nelson Keene, three solo singers who had all failed to achieve their expected sales – the group followed their example

The Fourmost outside London's fabled Palladium Theatre – their manager Brian Epstein had his office right next door!

THE FOURMOST

"We're not a rock'n'roll group, we play strictly rhythm and blues"
Mick Jagger, Jazz News

Like most of the Liverpool groups, London's Rolling Stones' debut disc was a cover of US material

Manchester's Hollies were writing their first entry in the chart log. Their first single was a revival of 'Just Like Me', an R&B song originally recorded by American vocal group The Coasters (who were also the inspiration for much of the Fourmost's on-stage material). Their first UK Top 20 entry was 'Searchin', a humorous detective ditty, which yet again The Coasters had originally taken up the US charts. The Manchester quintet followed this with a version of 'Stay', a song with which its composer, Maurice Williams, had a Stateside No. 1 with three years earlier. The Hollies followed this with a cover of Doris Troy's American hit 'Just

One Look' which gave them their Top 3 debut. From then on they seldom wandered into cover country, preferring to record songs written by them or especially for them. The Hollies are rightfully regarded as one of the most original and influential British groups of the era.

COVER VERSIONS

Record Mirror, which was fast gaining ground on the *NME* as Britain's No. 1 pop music paper, was concerned about the number of cover versions UK groups were releasing. It concluded 'British songs just aren't good enough,' noting 'in many cases the British records are not just copying the song, they are duplicating the whole arrangement and backing from the original American versions.' This praiseworthy publication went as far as saying 'The main reason the UK record is a hit, whereas the superior US version failed, is simply because the British artist appears on shows like *Thank Your Lucky Stars*.' They concluded with the hope that British songwriters would soon be producing songs that UK artists wanted to record in preference to covering American compositions.

Arguably the most covered American artist in the early Beat boom years was rock'n'roll idol Chuck Berry. This singer/songwriter, who was a virtual stranger to the UK charts during his US hey-day in the late 1950s, found his back catalogue raided by almost every would-be R&B group in the Britain. The Rolling Stones are among those that owe him a substantial debt, the London group having made their recording debut with Berry's 'Come On'. Both artists' versions sold well, with the Rolling Stones reaching the Top 20 singles, and Berry's original version being included on a Top 20 album. The Stones, who are considered by many to be the first genuine UK R&B act, added fuel to the North-South group battle when they scored their biggest success of 1963 with a treatment of Lennon & McCartney's 'I Wanna Be Your Man'.

Before this eventful and exciting musical year passed into history southern group Bern Elliott & The Fenmen, and long-time Merseyside favourites The Swinging Blue Jeans also made their UK Top 20 debuts. Elliott and his combo, veterans of the German club scene, scored with a UK-targeted treatment of Motown's first major US success, Barrett Strong's 'Money'. The Swinging Blue Jeans, who had earlier managed a week in the Top 30 with their own composition, 'It's Too Late Now', shot into the chart with a revival of 'Hippy Hippy Shake'. For the record, the inspiration for the song's unforgettable intro 'For goodness sake....', came from Nancy Kwan's often used phrase in the film *The World of Suzy Wong*. As 1963 drew to an end, many of the top groups were appearing in pantomime, the traditional British Christmastime stage show. The music may have changed, but it seemed the goals of the performers were the same as those of their Music Hall forebears earlier in the century – to entertain a wide family audience during the season of goodwill.

It had been an amazing year in many ways. Forty-seven groups reached the UK chart (36% of all hit acts), which was three times as many as the previous year. Only nine acts reached No. 1 and six of those made their Top 20 debuts in 1963. Just one-third of the songs that hit No. 1 were American; and for the first time in pop music history, all the year's chart topping acts had been British!

> Denny Laine & The Diplomats
> were playing the club circuit

A far cry from their be-jeaned days as a skiffle group, the neat-suited Swinging Blue Jeans

GERRY & THE PACEMAKERS

Liverpool born Gerry Marsden started playing in a skiffle group at his local youth club when he was just 14. In 1959 he formed Gerry Marsden & The Mars Bars, who became the Gerry Marsden Trio before settling on the name Gerry & The Pacemakers. In the early 1960s they became one of the most successful acts on Merseyside, and they often appeared with the area's other main attraction, The Beatles. Like their friends and rivals, Gerry & The Pacemakers spent many months honing their act in Hamburg cellar clubs in the early 1960s. In mid-1962 the group signed with Brian Epstein. He persuaded EMI producer George Martin to come to Liverpool and see them perform in front of their own fans at Top Rank's Majestic Ballroom (a venue that showcased 16 groups a week at the time). Martin was so impressed that he skipped the standard London audition, signed them to Columbia

Gerry Marsden (centre) with (left to right) Freddy Marsden, Les McGuire and Les Chadwick

Records and took them straight into the studio. A result of that first session was 'How Do You Do It' (a song previously recorded, but not released, by The Beatles), which zoomed right to the top of the UK chart. The single was also rush released in the USA, but it failed to generate any noticeable sales at the time. Gerry & The Pacemakers, who comprised Gerry (vocal, guitar), his elder brother Fred Marsden (drums), Les Maguire (piano) and Les Chadwick (bass), were voted Top New Act Of 1963 in the prestigious *NME* Readers Poll. Hit followed hit for the Pacemakers, with their revival of 'You'll Never Walk Alone' following 'I Like It' (previously recorded by the Dave Clark Five) into the coveted top spot. Barely seven months after making their Top 20 debut, they became the first act to top the UK chart with their initial three singles. The combo also raked up enviable album sales in 1963, when their debut set, How Do You Like It?, was only kept out of the pole position by The Beatles. The major professional ambition of Gerry & The Pacemakers had always been to become successful in the States, and in 1964 their

The Outlaws, which included later Deep Purple star Ritchie Blackmore, were on the road backing visiting US rockers Jerry Lee Lewis and Gene Vincent

wish came true when they helped spearhead the British Invasion. Not only did 'How Do You Do It' crack the American Top 10 but so did the group's composition 'Don't Let The Sun Catch You Crying' and Gerry's self-penned 'Ferry Cross The Mersey' (the title song from the film in which the group starred). In all, the quartet had 11 US chart entries and nine in the UK before they disbanded in 1967. Since then the effervescent lead singer, with the endless grin and unique guitar stance, has recorded as a soloist on a variety of labels. He has also appeared in a West End musical, been a successful children's TV personality and played the nostalgia circuit with a new line-up of Pacemakers. Gerry returned to the No. 1 spot in the UK in 1985 as lead vocalist of an all-star group called The Crowd, whose re-recording of 'You'll Never Walk Alone' raised money for families of the Bradford City Football Club fire victims. Gerry, who is one of the best-loved performers of the 1960s, was also the main vocalist on another celebrity packed charity chart-topper in 1989. It was a revival of his million selling transatlantic Top 10 hit, 'Ferry Cross The Mersey', the proceeds this time going to the relatives of 95 Liverpool fans crushed to death at the Hillsborough football disaster. Gerry & The Pacemakers were not only one of the flagships of Merseybeat, they were also the epitome of the Merseybeat sound.

BILLY J. KRAMER & THE DAKOTAS

Billy J. Kramer (born William Howard Ashton) was the youngest of seven children from Bootle, Lancashire, who with the help of a telephone operator chose his stage name from the phone directory. He first came to the attention of Brian Epstein when he was the lead singer of Liverpool combo The Coasters (also known at times as Billy Forde & The Phantoms). The group, who were regulars on the working men's club circuit in the Merseyside area, turned down the chance of backing Kramer full time. Therefore in February 1963, Epstein put the photogenic Kramer with Manchester band The Dakotas (so called because they originally dressed as Red Indians), who were looking for a lead singer to replace Pete Maclaine. Epstein quickly booked them into the famous Star Club in Hamburg to iron out any rough spots, before they went into the studio for Parlophone Records with producer George Martin. One of the first tracks they cut was 'Do You Want To Know A Secret', which went on to top the UK chart. Kramer said 'Lennon & McCartney wrote my first single for me some time before I recorded it, and I have been doing a slower version of it in the stage act for some time.' As his first release climbed the chart, Kramer quipped 'I don't want much out of life, just another hit record and fame in America!' That second hit came with a second made-to-measure Lennon & McCartney composition, 'Bad To Me' (which Lennon penned whilst on holiday in Spain with Epstein), which reached the No. 1 spot on Kramer's 20th birthday in August 1963. When speaking about his music, Kramer was adamant that he was a R&B performer, 'The fact that I include quite a bit of pop ballad material in my act, doesn't mean I'm not a part of the R& B field.' The Dakotas, whose initial line-up was Mike Maxfield (lead guitar), Robin McDonald (rhythm), Ray Jones (bass) and Tony Mansfield (drums)

In the year that groups finally found their feet in Britain, one of the biggest-selling were the decidedly dated and arguably racially offensive George Mitchell Minstrels

The nearest the Liverpool boom produced to a pre-beat type of 'good looking' pop idol was the photogenic Billy J. Kramer

also managed a UK Top 20 entry of their own in 1963 with 'The Cruel Sea'. Kramer won the *Melody Maker* poll as Best Newcomer of 1963 and went on to become one of the first artists to break down the doors of the US chart in 1964. The always well-groomed singer and his group scored their biggest American hit with their third and final British No. 1 'Little Children', penned for him by noted US rock'n'roll songwriter Mort Shuman. In all, Billy J. Kramer & The Dakotas had four US Top 40 entries in 1964, although their only other Top 10 single was a re-issue of 'Bad To Me' (which had been the B-side of 'Little Children'). After a run of five successive UK Top 20 singles, four of which Lennon & McCartney composed, his ironically titled 'It's Gotta Last Forever' failed to score. He returned to the Top 10 in 1965 with his next release, a cover of Burt Bacharach's 'Trains And Boats And Planes', but it was his last chart record on either side of the Atlantic. Kramer and the Dakotas went their separate ways in 1968. He has since recorded for over a dozen labels without success.

"I don't want much out of life, just another hit record and fame in America"

Billy J. Kramer

Sheet music sales, once the main barometer of a song's popularity, were still a factor in the Sixties

FREDDIE & THE DREAMERS

Madcap Mancunian Freddie Garrity began singing in the Red Sox Skiffle Group in the late 1950s. He later joined the John Norman Four and then The Kingfishers, who evolved into Freddie & The Dreamers. The group's line-up was Roy Crewsdon (guitar), Derek Quinn (guitar), Pete Birrell (bass) and Bernie Dwyer (drums). Whilst working the Northern clubs and various German venues, this very visual group built up a reputation as one of the zaniest combos around. Their first release 'If You Gotta Make A Fool Of Somebody', reached the Top 3, easily outselling another UK cover version by Buddy Britten & The Regents. The group's bespectacled, gnome-like front man co-wrote their equally successful follow-up, 'I'm Telling You Now', with top-notch writer Mitch Murray, who also penned their third major hit, 'You Were Made For Me'. All three of these singles also appeared on the quirky quintet's eponymous Top 5 debut album. The high kicking group with the high jumping, oft-giggling lead singer were naturals for pantomime, and they also appeared in a handful of 1960s pop movies. Whilst other UK acts were raking in American gold in 1964, Freddie & The Dreamers added to their British hit tally, with versions of Paul Anka's bouncy 'I Love You Baby', The G-Clef's 'I Understand' (originally recorded by doo-wop quartet The Four Tunes) and Dreamer Derek Quinn's composition 'Over You'. When America finally saw Freddie & The Dreamers in early 1965, it was love at first sight, and a re-issue of their 1963 US flop, 'I'm Telling You Now', quickly took them to the top there. It was, however, to be a short love affair, as the group only made one more trip into the American Top 20. Their final hit 'Do The Freddie' (about their agile stage routine), was especially written for them by US R&B artist Lou Courtney and noted tunesmith Dennis Lambert. By 1966, frantic Freddie's chapter in the History of Pop Music was completed, and he moved easily into a career in children's television and cabaret. Freddie & The Dreamers are often unfairly dismissed simply as a joke. They may have been a novelty act, but let's not forget that they were unique, and true entertainers.

BRIAN POOLE & THE TREMELOES

This Essex-based group, who were formed in 1959 as Brian Poole & The Tremilos (the name change occurring thanks to a record company mistake), started as Crickets-clones (Poole admitted 'I deliberately used to wear Buddy Holly glasses.') Decca Records A&R manager Mike Smith signed them in preference to The Beatles, whom he auditioned on the same day. Their line-up in 1962 at the time of their first single, 'Twist Little Sister', comprised Brian Poole (vocals), Rick West

> Island Records got their first
> mentions in the music press

Brian Poole and the boys in a typical Sixties pop pose in London's Hyde Park

(lead guitar), Alan Blakely (rhythm guitar), Alan Howard (bass) and Dave Munden (drums). Whilst waiting for a hit of their own, the group sang background vocals on recordings by such acts as Jet Harris, Tommy Steele, the Vernons Girls and disc-jockey Jimmy Savile. Their first chart success came with their fifth single, 'Twist & Shout', a fast live-sounding version of the well-known R&B song. Brian Poole &

The Tremeloes' biggest hit came with another track recorded at the same session, 'Do You Love Me'. On the album front, they released a collection of top-selling UK songs entitled Hitsville '62, and another of recent US successes (especially

A slightly later, mid-Sixties line-up of The Searchers, with (left to right) founders Pender and McNally and newcomers Johnny Blunt and Frank Allen

recorded for the Canadian market), before their cover version-crammed Twist & Shout album in 1963. The group returned to the UK Top 10 in 1964 with a Crickets B-side, 'Someone Someone' (Holly's mentor Norman Petty played the piano on it) and 'Candy Man' an earlier B-side by Roy Orbison (whom they supported on a 1963 UK tour). Despite their pre-eminence in Britain, the group never broke into the US market, and Poole and The Tremeloes went their separate ways in early 1966. Despite several attempts Poole was never to reach the heights again, but The Tremeloes still had their best years ahead of them.

"Until now a lot of the songs we record have been ignored in Britain, but we think the fans are beginning to realise how fabulous they are"

The Searchers

SEARCHERS
This Liverpool-based vocal/instrumental group were formed in 1961 to back Country-oriented performer Johnny Sandon, who left them a year later to set up the Remo Four. The Searchers,

34

who got their name from a John Wayne movie, consisted of Mike Pender (born Pendergast) an ex- member of The Wreckers and The Confederates (lead guitar), Tony Jackson (bass), John McNally (rhythm guitar) and Chris Curtis (drums). In 1962 the quartet, whose vocal harmonies set them apart from most other UK groups of the era, were regulars at Liverpool's Iron Door club and appeared successfully at the Star Club in Hamburg. Their first single, a revival of The Drifters' 1961 US Top 20 entry, 'Sweets For My Sweet', topped the British chart. The group were big fans of American R&B songs, and they included many on their debut LP, Meet The Searchers, which only The Beatles prevented from reaching No. 1. The Searchers helped introduce the UK public to many great, hitherto unknown, American compositions. 'Until now a lot of the songs we record have been ignored in Britain, but we think the fans are beginning to realise how fabulous they are,' the group proudly announced. Among the lesser known US songs they recorded were their two 1964 chart toppers 'Needles and Pins' (previously cut by Jackie DeShannon) and 'Don't Throw Your Love Away' (first released by The Orlons). Over the next two years, they racked up 10 UK Top 20 hits (most of which, yet again, introduced the British audience to little-known American songs) and four Top 10 albums. The Searchers were also highly regarded in the USA, where they had three Top 20 hits. Their biggest Stateside single was a revival of 'Love Potion No. 9' (a 1959 US chart entry for The Clovers), which was never released as a single in Britain. This innovative and vocally influential group are considered to be seminal figures in the folk-rock movement. The Searchers, who later recorded with minimal success for labels such as RCA, Liberty and Sire, remain a major attraction on the cabaret circuit.

The Fourmost (below) like many of their contemporaries, ended up on the Northern cabaret club circuit for many years

The first black vocal group from Liverpool, The Chants, included Eddie Amoo, later in The Real Thing

FOURMOST

Brian O'Hara (guitar, vocals) and Billy Hatton (bass) formed the Blue Jays whilst still at school. Four years later in 1962, Mike Millward (guitar, vocals) and Dave Lovelady (drums) joined the line-up, and the group became the Four Mosts. In mid-1963 Brian Epstein took over the reins, slightly amended their name, and signed them to Parlophone. No doubt partly because of Epstein's influence, John Lennon & Paul McCartney allowed the quartet to release the first recordings of two of their compositions, 'Hello Little Girl' (a number the Beatles often sang at the Cavern before success came their way) and 'I'm In Love', both of which reached the UK Top 20. The group, acknowledged as one of the zaniest bands on the scene, had the biggest hit of their career in May '64 with the Russell Alquist Jr. composition, 'A Little Loving'. This single peaked at No. 6, as they began an eight-month residency at the prestigious London Palladium, supporting fellow Liverpudlians Frankie Vaughan and Cilla Black. The Fourmost were an archetypal Merseyside group, whose star began to fade as the basic Liverpool sound lost its appeal. Their last Top 30 entry came with a brave cover of the Four Tops US hit 'Baby I Need Your Loving', which easily outpaced the original version in the UK. Despite a cameo appearance in the Gerry & The Pacemakers film, *Ferry Cross The Mersey*, the group achieved no noticeable sales in the USA. Millward died of leukaemia aged 23 in 1966, by which time The Fourmost's fan following had fizzled out, and their days as chart regulars were already over.

HOLLIES

The Hollies were one of the most enduring groups to emerge from the British Beat Boom, and the 1993 version of the band still included three long-serving members: original vocalist Allan Clarke (who later made a solo album My Real Name is

Making it big down the 'Smoke' – Manchester's Hollies outside Buckingham Palace

The Hollies (left to right) Alan
Clarke, Bobby Elliott, Graham Nash,
Eric Haydock and Tony Hicks

Harold - which it is) and fellow founder and lead guitarist Tony Hicks, along with drummer Bobby Elliott, who joined from Shane Fenton's Fentones when Don Rathbone, an original member, left in 1963. Hicks was the only newcomer when Clarke, Rathbone, singer/guitarist Graham Nash and bass player Eric Haydock changed the name of their group from The Deltas to the Hollies. Their first four UK hits were all versions of US R&B songs, and it soon became clear that long term success would be more likely if they could discover a more original source of material. Since both The Beatles and Stones were writing their own hits, Clarke and Nash, who had performed together as a vocal duo in the style of the Everly Brothers, added Hicks to become a songwriting team known by the fictitious name of L. Ransford. This trio's three-part harmonies gave the group a distinctive sound which has never really been equalled, although their musical direction evolved away from R&B towards pop, both through Ransford-penned originals such as 'Stop Stop Stop', 'On A Carousel' and 'Carrie-Anne' (all of which reached the US Top 20), hits like 'Bus Stop' (their first US Top 20 entry) and 'Look Through Any Window', which were written by fellow Mancunian Graham Gouldman (later of 10cc). Ironically, their only UK chart-toppers of the 1960s were with American songs 'I'm Alive', a Clint Ballard composition that Wayne Fontana had turned

1963
TOP SINGLES ARTISTS IN THE UK

1. **THE BEATLES**
   PARLOPHONE *UK*

2. **CLIFF RICHARD**
   COLUMBIA *UK*

3. **THE SHADOWS**
   COLUMBIA *UK*

4. **GERRY & THE PACEMAKERS**
   COLUMBIA *UK*

5. **FRANK IFIELD**
   COLUMBIA *UK*

6. **BILLY J. KRAMER & THE DAKOTAS**
   PARLOPHONE *UK*

7. **JET HARRIS & TONY MEEHAN**
   DECCA *UK*

8. **FREDDIE & THE DREAMERS**
   COLUMBIA *UK*

9. **BILLY FURY**
   DECCA *UK*

10. **ROY ORBISON**
    LONDON AMERICAN *US*

11. **THE SEARCHERS**
    PYE *UK*

12. **BRIAN POOLE & THE TREMELOES**
    DECCA *UK*

13. **THE CRYSTALS**
    LONDON AMERICAN *US*

14. **DEL SHANNON**
    LONDON AMERICAN *US*

15. **ELVIS PRESLEY**
    RCA *US*

16. **BUDDY HOLLY**
    CORAL *US*

17. **THE TORNADOS**
    DECCA *UK*

18. **THE SPRINGFIELDS**
    PHILIPS *UK*

19. **JOE BROWN & THE BRUVVERS**
    PICCADILLY *UK*

20. **KATHY KIRBY**
    DECCA *UK*

down and 'I Can't Let Go', written by Chip Taylor (best known for writing 'Wild Thing'). The Hollies were spectacularly successful throughout the 1960s when they had 19 UK and 5 US Top 20 singles and 6 UK and 1 US Top 20 album. Surprisingly the group returned to the top of the UK singles chart in 1988 with their 1969 recording 'He Ain't Heavy, He's My Brother' which was being used in a television commercial.

SWINGING BLUE JEANS

The Swinging Blue Jeans evolved from an amateur skiffle group first formed in 1957 by Liverpudlians Ray Ennis (lead guitar/vocals) and Norman Kuhlke (washboard/drums). Ralph Ellis (rhythm guitar/vocals) was recruited from another local skiffle group in 1958, and a year later Les Braid (bass) joined the group, who were then known as The Bluegenes Skiffle Group. They became regulars at the Cavern Club (The Beatles made their first appearance there as guests of the Bluegenes) and like many other Merseyside bands in the early 1960s, found themselves flitting between Liverpool and Hamburg. After an unsuccessful audition for Joe Meek and a fruitless spell with Oriole Records (who dropped their contract because they were 'amateurish and unprofessional'), the quartet, now known as The Swinging Blue Jeans (originally spelt Swinging Bluegenes), joined the HMV label in 1963. Before long they signed a deal with the denim manufacturer Lybro, who sponsored the group's regular Radio Luxembourg show. Ironically, at that stage of their career the group, who were then in their early twenties, felt 'we're getting too old to actually wear jeans.' Their debut single 'It's Too late Now' was a minor hit, and Tina Robin covered it in America. Their third release, 'Hippy Hippy Shake', which took only 30 minutes to record, took them into the Top 3. The following year it also made the US Top 40, a feat the original American version by composer Chan Romero had failed to achieve. The group had two major hits in 1964, with interpretations of Little Richard's classic 'Good Golly Miss Molly', and Betty Everett's US R&B success 'You're No Good'. After that, record buyers gave them the thumbs down - the public's musical tastes had moved on. Nonetheless, like many of their Merseyside contemporaries, the group's undoubted nostalgia value remains bankable.

BIG THREE

In 1962, this much-heralded Merseyside trio comprised Johnny Gustafson (bass, vocals) Johnny Hutchinson (drums, vocal) and Brian Griffiths (guitar). The group, who had previously worked with Brian Casser as Cass & The Casanovas, claimed to have been the first beat group in Liverpool. They reached near-legendary status on Merseyside and in Hamburg before signing with Brian Epstein in 1962, and Decca shortly afterwards. Their future looked bright. However, the Big Three's debut single, a revival of 'Some Other Guy', by US R&B singer Ritchie Barrett (later the Three Degrees manager), was only a medium seller. Their only chart entry came in mid-1963, when their recording of Mitch Murray's 'By The Way' just cracked the Top 30. The trio, whose live EP At The Cavern received much critical acclaim, disbanded at the end of 1963, shortly after leaving the Brian Epstein stable for the Manchester-based Kennedy Street Management . Gustafson then joined The Merseybeats, and during the Seventies was a member of Roxy Music for a time.

OTHER 1963 RELEASES

Among the groups who made unsuccessful recording debuts in Britain in 1963 were later hit makers: The Barron Knights, Wayne Gibson & The Dynamic Sounds, The Fortunes (then a trio consisting of ex members of Robby Hood &

The Merrymen), The Mojos, Manfred Mann, The Rockin' Berries, Wayne Fontana & The Mindbenders, The Merseybeats, The Migil 5 and The Overlanders. Other interesting releases that year included singles by: Casey Jones (a one-time stunt man who had appeared in over 50 films) & The Engineers, a group which included pianist Nicky Hopkins and at times Eric Clapton (before The Yardbirds, John Mayall, Cream, Blind Faith and so on) & Tom McGuinness (Manfred Mann/McGuinness Flint/The Blues Band), The Cheynes (who included Mick Fleetwood), Wes Sands (later a hit maker as Richard Sarstedt), Liverpool's Freddie Starr & The Midnighters, The Moontrekkers (with whom Rod Stewart sang), The Paramounts (who evolved into Procol Harum), Neil Christian & The Crusaders (a group in which Jimmy Page played). Sixteen year old Steve Marriott (later of the Small Faces and Humble Pie) released his first single, 'Give Her My Regards'. In August, the actor Tom Courtenay released 'Mrs. Brown You Have A Lovely Daughter', one of five songs especially written for his TV play *The Lads* by Trevor Peacock (who sang it in the play). Despite an appearance on top television programme *Ready Steady Go*, Courtenay's record sank without trace. The song, of course, later topped the American chart in a version by Herman's Hermits.

The Swinging Blue Jeans were typical of many Beat Boom groups who failed to progress into the latter part of the decade

1963 TOP SINGLES IN THE UK

	TITLE	ARTIST
1	SHE LOVES YOU	THE BEATLES
2	FROM ME TO YOU	THE BEATLES
3	I WANT TO HOLD YOUR HAND	THE BEATLES
4	I LIKE IT	GERRY & THE PACEMAKERS
5	DO YOU LOVE ME	BRIAN POOLE & THE TREMELOES
6	YOU'LL NEVER WALK ALONE	GERRY & THE PACEMAKERS
7	DIAMONDS	JET HARRIS & TONY MEEHAN
8	HOW DO YOU DO IT	GERRY & THE PACEMAKERS
9	CONFESSIN'	FRANK IFIELD
10	SWEETS FOR MY SWEET	THE SEARCHERS
11	SUMMER HOLIDAY	CLIFF RICHARD
12	DANCE ON	THE SHADOWS
13	PLEASE PLEASE ME	THE BEATLES
14	BAD TO ME	BILLY J. KRAMER & THE DAKOTAS
15	DO YOU WANT TO KNOW A SECRET	BILLY J. KRAMER & THE DAKOTAS
16	WAYWARD WIND	FRANK IFIELD
17	FOOT TAPPER	THE SHADOWS
18	FROM A JACK TO A KING	NED MILLER
19	ATLANTIS	THE SHADOWS
20	SCARLETT O'HARA	JET HARRIS & TONY MEEHAN

The british invasion
- an overview

The assassination of America's beloved president, John F. Kennedy, in late November, 1963, put the world's mightiest nation into mourning. A grieving public was gently eased into the New Year by the soothing, sweet and innocent voice of a Belgian Nun, Jeanine Deckers, known simply as The Singing Nun or Soeur Sourire ('Sister Smile'). Her composition, 'Dominique', was the most listened to song in the USA as 1963 drew to a close, while in those first weeks after the brutal murder, her self-titled album was outselling everything else. At that unforgettable moment in history, few could have foreseen that in just a matter of days the British would mount an invasion on the United States, the likes of which had not been seen since the American War of Independence nearly 200 years earlier, when the despised 'redcoats' were defeated and despatched back across the Atlantic.

To say that this was a surprise attack would be an understatement on an enormous scale. There appeared to be no advance warning and no tell-tale signs – unless you count the presence of the plaintive British female duo The Caravelles and their cutesy 'You Don't Have To Be A Baby To Cry' in the American Top 10 singles. It is true that in 1963, group-mania gripped Britain for the first time. The Beatles, a long-haired strangely garbed group from the unfashionable city of Liverpool had started the craze, and during the year around a dozen other groups had joined them. Understandably, though, this was not taken as a sign that Britain was preparing itself to take on the might of America in a head-to-head battle over rock supremacy. After all, Britain had a history of localised and short-lived musical

Motown vocal group
The Supremes released
an album called
A Bit Of Liverpool

The Singing Nun, with an unidentified colleague, inside her convent at Pichermont, Belgium, during the taping of a sequence for the *Ed Sullivan Show*

crazes. Consider the previous few years, when the UK had gone skiffle mad and had then embraced traditional jazz with equal fervour. From the former craze, only Lonnie Donegan's 'Rock Island Line' and 'Does Your Chewing Gum Lose Its Flavour' had meant much in the US, and although British trad performers Chris Barber, Kenny Ball and Acker Bilk had all reached the US Top 10, nothing even remotely resembling a craze had started in the land which had invented and discarded trad decades earlier. To the trained observer, this British group phenomenon was nothing more than another UK-only craze, which at best might result in a couple of acts having one-off hits in the US, the country which had always set pop policies for the world. In retrospect, perhaps more notice should have been taken of *Billboard* magazine's 1963 International record survey. This showed that not only had Cliff Richard replaced Elvis as the world's most popular singer, but also nine of the World's Top 20 acts hailed from Britain. As it happened, the survey caused no more than a ripple Stateside, where the tastes of much smaller record markets were not considered important. If more proof were needed that British acts were still far from ready to take their place in world class rock, a quick glance would show most of their hits were covers of US records. Only a couple of the UK acts recorded British songs, with just one of them, The Beatles, hitting regularly with original material – although they too relied heavily on American songs on stage and on their albums. On the face of it, there were just not enough original artists and ideas on the British music scene to worry their American counterparts. If you still think someone in America should have noticed the overseas threat, then remember many of these British hits, including some by The Beatles,

> **Even the studio-created Chipmunks got in on the Brit act with their Sing The Beatles' Hits album**

The US Vee Jay label released a documentary LP entitled *Songs Pictures and Stories of the Fabulous Beatles*

The Beatles, backs to the camera, face the American media in their first ever press conference on landing in New York City

had already been released and failed miserably in America. In fact, Capitol Records, their label's US outlet, thought so little of The Beatles' big British hits that they had rejected them altogether and allowed other US labels to release their singles.

To appreciate fully the enormity of the attack, as well as its totally unexpected nature, we should look at the success of previous raids on the US chart by British acts. In the first nine years of rock music, only 15 UK-produced records managed to climb into the US Top 20. These were a mixture of trad, skiffle, pop and MOR records, with only The Tornados instrumental novelty hit, 'Telstar', fitting the description of beat or rock music. For the record, the total number of singles reaching the US Top 20 in that period was 1187; or to put it mathematically, British acts only accounted for 1.25% of major US hits before 1964! This lowly figure increased to an amazing 26% in the first year of the British invasion.

"Great Britain has not been as influential in American affairs since 1775"

Billboard

THE MOP TOPS

The Beatles spearheaded the attack. Their campaign was costly, and was as carefully and strategically planned as any battle. The initial aim of the massive publicity machine supporting them was to ensure that within a matter of days, most Americans could not only read about Beatlemania, but see it in action in their homes. Before the group had even entered the US Top 100, *Time*, *Life* and *Newsweek* featured articles on them, while The Jack Paar Show and the top two news programmes, *CBS TV's Walter Cronkite News* and *NBC-TV's Huntley-Brinkley News,* included film of live UK performances. A double-page advertisement (a rare event in itself) in the American music trade papers *Billboard* and *Cash Box* warned dealers, 'Be prepared for the kind of sales epidemic that made The Beatles the biggest selling vocal group in British history.' The pre-release hype was so heavy the act, whose first three American releases had hardly sold past double figures, were booked on two consecutive Ed Sullivan shows, even before the release of their first US hit. The record receiving this prodigious push was the group's fifth British single, 'I Want To Hold Your Hand'.

The Beatles fired the opening shots of the British Invasion on January 18, 1964, a day that will stand in infamy for the many American pop acts who, from then on, found their way into the charts barred by the British. 'I Want To Hold Your Hand' entered the Top 100 at No. 45, and after this respectable start, leapt to No. 3 and then to the top spot − a place it still held when the group appeared on the *Ed Sullivan Show* (seen by a record 73 million people) on February 9. On returning to the show a week later, their debut album, Meet The Beatles, was also topping the chart.

The success of The Beatles in America came like a bolt out of the blue to the UK's music industry and press. Apart from Brian Epstein, it appeared that few people 'in the know' were confident Beatlemania would grip America with anything like the ferocity it had in the group's homeland. The only people not surprised by the events were the group's millions of British fans − who already knew The Beatles were 'the best group in the world'.

GOLD RUSH

While Capitol Records marshalled their troops behind The Beatles, their rivals Columbia (CBS) made it a two-pronged attack by giving their support, albeit more modestly, to another British outfit, The Dave Clark Five. Suddenly, Liverpool and London were hip cities to hail from, although in the early days of the invasion, they were sometimes confused. For instance, *Billboard* magazine described The Beatles as having 'a surf on the Thames sound' (the London river) and said the Dave Clark Five had 'The Mersey Sound With The Liverpool Beat', a fact greatly annoying to Londoner Clark.

Once the US record business came to realise that transatlantic hits were no longer a one-way process, it quickly and adeptly adjusted to the situation. The British gold rush was on − with American record companies either battling each other for the rights to current British hits, or quickly re-issuing 1963 UK chart successes which had fallen on stony ground when they were first released in the USA less than a year earlier.

"A surf on the

Thames sound"

Billboard on

The Beatles

Despite his unlikely image, Ed Sullivan, through his TV show, was a prime promoter of the British Invasion groups

"The Mersey

Sound with the

Liverpool Beat"

Billboard on The

Dave Clark Five

Battalions of British groups followed The Beatles into the US chart, once the 'mop tops' had broken down the barricades that had kept out foreign invaders for so long. *Billboard* was quick to notice 'the redcoats are widening their beachhead', adding 'Great Britain has not been as influential in American affairs since 1775.' On the first American Independence Day since the triumphant return of the British, five of the Top 10 singles in the USA were by UK performers, and US TV variety shows were falling over themselves to feature British artists. Before the year was out, four dozen UK records had breached the Top 20 – over three times the total amount which had hit that target between 1955-63! It was not just the British big guns who were shooting up the US chart. Chad & Jeremy, Ian Whitcomb and The Hullaballoos, none of whom meant much in their homeland, were creating a hullabaloo in the birthplace of rock. Perhaps the most astounding thing about this

"The redcoats are widening their beachhead"

Billboard

Never that big in their homeland, Chad Stuart (left) and Jeremy Clyde were huge in the 'States

invasion was many of the British groups were aiming successfully at the charts with bullets manufactured in the USA – that is to say songs written in America and originally performed by Americans. Suddenly the US public was accepting almost anything sung by a British act, and were by and large unaware that they had ignored the often superior original versions of the same song performed by their compatriots. For years British cover versions of American records had not even merited a US release, but now they were charting week after week. The 'redcoats' had returned with a musical vengeance and the American rock scene would never be the same again.

The british are coming

1964 – THE GREAT INVASION

The Beatles held the top two positions on the UK album chart for the first four months of 1964, and as the year opened, only the Dave Clark Five's 'Glad All Over' prevented them from hogging the top two places on the singles chart as well. The North London-based Dave Clark Five were the hottest new act of the period. Their scintillating stomper, 'Glad All Over', sold almost a million in the UK alone, while the follow-up, 'Bits & Pieces', amassed advance orders of over 250,000 and almost gave the well turned-out combo another chart topper. Photogenic drummer Clark, together with the band's strong voiced keyboard playing lead singer Mike Smith, wrote these anthemic hits, which are arguably best remembered for their ultra-heavy bass drum sound (reputedly based on an idea borrowed from producer Joe Meek). Clark disliked being likened to the Liverpool groups, 'I don't know what the Mersey sound is' he stated, 'But I do know we're nothing like The Beatles or Gerry, or any others from the North. Our backing is much bigger, after all we're got saxophone and organ.' The group were also enormously successful in America, where their appearances caused pandemonium. A New York reviewer said of them,'They have considerably more volume than The Beatles – and so have their fans.'

The next new British group to make their mark on both sides of the Atlantic was Manfred Mann, a R&B quintet named after their bearded organ-playing leader. Their third release, '5-4-3-2-1' (the theme song to top TV series *Ready Steady Go*), became the first of 17 UK Top 10 singles accumulated by the group. Manfred Mann, whose initial hits featured vocalist Paul Jones, scored again with another self-composed song, 'Hubble Bubble Toil And Trouble', before striking gold with the John Burgess-produced transatlantic chart topper, 'Do Wah Diddy

Smooth-looking Dave Clark (below) was another invader who meant more in the US than in his native UK – though he did score several times in the British charts

"I don't know what the Mersey Sound is, but I do know we're nothing like The Beatles or Gerry, or any others from the North. Our backing is much bigger, after all we've got saxophone and organ"

Dave Clark

Manfred Mann on piano with
(left to right) Mike Vickers,
Paul Jones, Tom McGuinness
and Mike Hugg

Diddy'. The distinctive act's only other US Top 20 entry came with their next release, 'Sha La La'. Incidentally, both records were covers of minor US hits, The Exciters having originally cut the former song and The Shirelles the latter.

HOMELAND HEROES

The first few months of 1964 not only signalled the start of the British invasion in the USA, they were also an extremely exciting period in Britain. Bluebeat, which was very popular with the Mods, was being tipped as the next musical craze, and for a while sales of the West Indian-originated music were most impressive. The top sellers included Prince Buster's 'Madness', after which one of the top groups of the 1980s named themselves, and 'Carolina' by The Folk Brothers, a song that topped the UK chart in 1993 by Shaggy. Genuine R&B was also selling in enviable quantities and Mods, who were now making regular trips to British coastal resorts to fight their enemies, the Rockers, were snapping up releases on the specialist R&B label Sue. The first pirate radio ship, Radio Caroline, was launched and at last Britain knew what it was like to have its own Top 40 station. Also for the first time British artists were making records with America in mind, since their wares were no longer automatically excluded from the US airwaves. March brought another first, when British acts held all the Top 10 places on the UK chart – in fact it was an all-British Top 14! Britain was starting to swing and everyone in the music business wanted to be a part of it. Spring 1964 found pop/MOR trio The Bachelors (who despite their dated sound, were one of the most successful groups of the Beat Boom era) taking up two slots in the UK Top 10, whilst the 'fabulous four' hogged all the fabulous five positions at the top of the US singles chart.

The success of The Beatles in Amercia meant that overnight British music gained a respectability and importance it had never previously come close to attaining. The UK media did an about-turn, acting as if they knew all along that The Beatles had the talent to crack the world's biggest record market. To ensure they

'Kinky Boots' by TV Avengers Patrick McNee and Honor Blackman released – it made the UK chart 26 years later!

were not caught out again, the British music press began to shower praise on almost every new group appearing in the Top 10.

Hit British recording artists were now being hailed as heroes in their homeland. They were also the recipients of the kind of attention in the USA that months earlier would have seemed absolutely impossible. This, however, did not mean every successful new British act cracked the American charts. Among those groups whose UK hits died in the USA were The Merseybeats, The Mojos, The Applejacks, the Migil Five and The Four Pennies.

FLEETING FAME

The Merseybeats, whose female fan following was large and loud, were the possessors of one of the corniest names and best sounds of the year. The group hit the Top 20 with two Peter Lee Stirling songs, 'I Think Of You' and 'Don't Turn Around', and with their interpretation of the compelling Bacharach and David composition, 'Wishin' And Hopin''. Amid all this success founder member Billy Kinsley announced his departure, 'It's pointless playing to people who scream and shout and won't listen' he complained. Kinsley returned to the group ironically in time to see the interest in them cool.

The Mojos from Liverpool, originally known as The Nomads, signed to Decca after lead vocalist Stu James (Stuart Slater) had won an important songwriting competition. Their only major chart success came with their second single, the self-composed 'Everything's Alright', which graced the UK Top 10 in mid-1964. The Mojos, whose hit is considered a 1960s classic, stopped working together in late 1966. James later married singer Stephanie DeSykes, and is now one of Britain's

Vocal group The Batchelors (above) were a smooth-sounding antidote to the dominance of guitar-based groups.
Below, The Merseybeats with replacement bass player Johnny Gustafson (right)

"It's pointless playing to people who scream and shout and won't listen"

Billy Kinsley

The Merseybeats

top music publishing executives. A later member of the group, bass player Bill (Lewis) Collins, subsequently found fame as an actor starring in programmes such as *The Professionals*.

Youthful Birmingham sextet The Applejacks were also unable to build on their initial success. Al Jackson fronted the clean-cut combo, which started as an instrumental group working under the names The Crestas and The Jaguars. Despite the fact the group were 'determined not to be one-hit wonders', only the catchy Geoff Stevens and Les Reed song, 'Tell Me When', took them to the upper reaches of

They all had their (albeit brief) moment of fame – top to bottom, The Mojos, The Applejacks and The Four Pennies

One-hit wonders The Migil Five (left) failed to make the sort of impression Stateside that was enjoyed by groups like The Zombies (below)

the chart. The Applejacks also included two Sunday school teachers, female bass player Megan Davies and drummer Gerry Freeman, who married shortly after their version of Lennon & McCartney's 'Like Dreamers Do' failed to emulate the success of their first release (although it did chart).

INTO SOMETHING GOOD

Top trad man Kenny Ball helped the one-time jazz trio the Migil Five land a deal with Pye Records. The London band's five minutes of fame came when their pop/blue beat revival of 'Mockingbird Hill' (a song which had been an early fifties success for both Patti Page and Les Paul & Mary Ford) flew into the Top 10. Before vanishing into the cabaret circuit, the group, named after members Mi(ke) Staples and Gil Lucas, had a minor hit with their follow-up, the late 1940s favourite, 'Near You'.

Talented Lancashire quartet The Four Pennies, whose plaintive and haunting ballad, 'Juliet', topped the UK chart, were another outfit that failed to join the British Invasion. The group, who relied heavily on distinctive lead singer Lionel Morton, found themselves splashed all over the UK tabloids and hailed as 'the next big thing', when they hit the No. 1 spot with their debut hit. Despite being one of the most original British groups of the time, their subsequent singles proved less fruitful, and they disbanded in 1966 when their pennies were running out.

Several sages, who had not foreseen the coming British Invasion, prophesied that it was impossible for the UK to keep up its supply of high standard groups. Nevertheless, as the months passed the list of transatlantic hit-makers grew, with the fall seeing the rise in the USA of not only major artists Herman's Hermits, The Animals, The Kinks and The Zombies, but also one-hit wonders The Nashville Teens and The Honeycombs.

Herman's Hermits were arguably second only to The Beatles in the hearts of American teenage girls in the mid-1960s, although, unlike their Liverpool rivals, they did not have the Midas touch when it came to composing their own hits. Therefore, much credit for their continued success should be shared with their producer Mickie Most. Most not only selected the right songs to record, but also knew which of these would be best suited for their US fans, and which ones his British followers would prefer. The group's debut disc, 'I'm Into Something Good', topped the British chart giving imp-like 16 year old Peter 'Herman' Noone and his clean-cut companions the first of their 14 American and 15 UK Top 20 singles. This amiable and wholesome group appealed not only to teenagers but also to their parents. From the start Noone knew his potential audience. 'On stage I make myself look as young as possible' he confided, 'and then all the girls in the audience go "aahh, isn't he nice".' Noone brought out the mothering instinct in his fans by playing on his 'little boy lost' image, and the group's sales of over 40 million records verify that this was an astute move. In 1965, at the height of 'Hermania' in America, the group amassed 600,000 advance orders for their version of 'Mrs. Brown You've Got A Lovely Daughter', a music hall styled song which entered the US Top 100 at No. 12, a feat not bettered by The Beatles at the time. Incidentally, they recorded this song (which had been featured in their stage act for some time) in just 10 minutes at the end of an album session. Herman's Hermits may have been a lightweight pop group – but they were heavyweights in that lucrative field.

"On stage I make myself look as young as possible and then all the girls in the audience go 'aaah, isn't he nice' "

Peter Noone

The Kinks (opposite page, left to right) Peter Quaife, Dave Davies, Mike Avory and Ray Davies

YOU REALLY GOT ME

The second British group to top the US charts was Newcastle combo The Animals, whose second single, 'House Of The Rising Sun', was a transatlantic No. 1 in 1964. The song was an old blues number which keyboard player Alan Price had rearranged, 'We couldn't use the original words' Price went on to explain, 'because they'd be too strong. What we did was change it from being about a house of ill repute to a story of a boy who loses all his money in a gambling house.' The Animals were hailed as the best British R&B act since the Rolling Stones. As it happens, the latter group's lead vocalist Mick Jagger was not overly impressed by 'House Of The Rising Sun'. 'It's no more R&B than how's-your-father!' Jagger said, adding 'personally I like the Bob Dylan version.' The first overseas tour by The Animals was in Japan. They followed this visit to the land of the rising sun with a trip to the home country of R&B, where New York welcomed them with a motorcade. The group headlined at the prestigious Paramount Theatre in Brooklyn (where Alan Freed held many of his great rock'n'roll shows) for 10 days, and they appeared on Ed Sullivan's top-rated TV show. Despite this, their first US visit was not a complete success, as they played to less than half empty houses at several poorly promoted shows. Despite this, The Animals came back raving about the potential of British groups in the USA, 'Americans are absolutely mad for our acts' they announced, 'There's a big future there for them.'

Controversy and The Kinks have often been close companions. When the group first burst onto the recording scene with their heavily hyped revival of Little Richard's classic, 'Long Tall Sally', posters screamed out 'If you like the Stones you'll love The Kinks.' This exorbitant claim was not, however, born out by the sales of their first two singles. Initially there appeared to be more interest in the sex

The Animals (left to right) Alan Price, Chas Chandler, John Steel, Eric Burdon and Hilton Valentine

"It's no more R'n'B than how's your father"

Mick Jagger on 'House of the Rising Sun'

of the group's very long haired clean-shaven lead guitarist (Dave Davies) than in their records. The Kinks' debut hit came with 'You Really Got Me' which according to its composer, the group's lead singer Ray Davies, had started out as a light jazzy tune before The Kinks gave it the 'Louie Louie' treatment. This classic record and its similar sounding follow-up, 'All Day And All Of The Night' (which surely inspired The Doors to pen 'Hello I Love You'), helped lay the foundations of the heavy metal guitar sound. Time has proved The Kinks to be one of the most original and successful recording acts of the rock era, and there is no doubt that British pop music would have been much the poorer without the songs of the perceptive and prolific Ray Davies.

Although St. Albans quintet The Zombies only recorded for a short time in comparison to The Kinks, they made a relatively big impression on the American music scene. The musically adventurous quintet from St. Albans (just north of London) first met when they were students at the local grammar school. In actuality, The Zombies, by comparison with many other Beat Boom bands, were so well-educated that at one time they were publicised as the group with more examination qualifications than any other. They were fronted by charismatic lead vocalist Colin Blunstone, who had the purity of voice of a choirboy, and their recordings also prominently featured the talents of keyboard player/songwriter Rod Argent. In 1964 the group's debut disc on the Decca label, the hauntingly memorable 'She's Not There', peaked just outside the British Top 10, but was a huge hit in the United States, reaching

As Davy Jones, the future David Bowie had his first write-up in the British music press

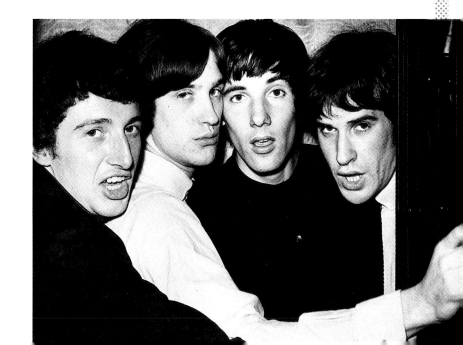

After first making a name for themselves as a backing band for American stars visiting Europe, The Nashville Teens soon broke through in their own right

the Top 3. Their second single, another magnetic Argent song 'Tell Her No', followed it into the US Top 10, but floundered outside the British chart. After such an auspicious Stateside start, sales of The Zombies records tailed off, and in 1967 after their tenth Decca single they signed to CBS. The combo cut a final album, the innovative Odessey And Oracle (sic), but broke up before it was released. In early 1969, Blunstone took his re-recorded version of 'She's Not There' into the UK Top 30 (under the name Neil MacArthur), and Argent formed a group simply called Argent with two ex-members of The Roulettes (once Adam Faith's backing group). Also that year, much to The Zombies' amazement, 'Time Of The Season', a Rod Argent composed track from their 1967 CBS album, returned the then defunct group into the US Top 3. Despite offers to tour should they wish to reform, the group members decided, perhaps wisely, not to bring The Zombies back to life and to concentrate on new ventures. Both Blunstone and Argent had solo success in the 1970s.

NASHVILLE, SURREY

The visually striking pair Ray Phillips and Arthur 'Artt' Sharp fronted The Nashville Teens. The Surrey sextet first recorded as the backing group to Jerry Lee Lewis on his live album from Hamburg's Star Club. The group's versions of Nashville songwriter John D. Loudermilk's 'Tobacco Road' and 'Google Eye' gave them consecutive British Top 20 hits with their first two singles. They felt their name might cause problems in the US, commenting, 'It's a bit like people over here having to accept an American group called the Merseymen.' They need not have worried as their debut disc did crack the American Top 20. However, after leaving producer Mickie Most in 1964, their big hits stopped on both sides of the Atlantic. The Nashville Teens recorded without success on several labels in the 1970s, and in the late 1980s Ray Phillips fronted the British Invasion All Stars, an ersatz supergroup who toured the USA on the 25th anniversary of the British invasion.

A TASTE OF HONEY

Another group receiving countless column inches in the daily papers was The Honeycombs. The reason for the interest, apart from the fact they had a No. 1 hit, was that they included a girl drummer, Annie 'Honey' Lantree. The Essex based group, formed by rhythm guitarist Martin Murray and fronted by singer Dennis D'Ell, also included Honey's brother, John, on bass. Originally known as The Sheratons, they changed their name shortly after Honey joined. After a slow start their debut single, 'Have I The Right', produced by Joe Meek and written by their managers Ken Howard and Howard Blaikley (who later wrote a string of UK hits for Dave Dee, Dozy, Beaky, Mick & Titch), shot to the top of the UK chart and into the American Top 5. The Honeycombs received more than their share of knocks, being accused, among other things, of sounding like a cross between Meek's act The Tornados (of 'Telstar' fame) and The Dave Clark Five. Martin admitted their hit did have a Dave Clark 'tramping' sound, but added 'there wasn't much else you could do with that number.' The quintet, who were adamant 'We're not a beat group, we're a beat ballad group', never again trampled up the US chart. although they did return, albeit briefly, to the UK Top 20 in 1965 with 'That's The Way'.

The saying 'humour doesn't travel well' is especially true in the case of British comedy on record travelling across the Atlantic. One case in point is that of the Barron Knights, a group who have put seven singles into the UK Top 20. This

"We're not a beat group, we're a beat ballad group" Martin Murray, The Honeycombs

Game for a laugh: The Barron Knights' comedy hits secured them a long-lasting career in cabaret long after their charting days were over

quirky quintet from Leighton Buzzard, Bedfordshire, specialised in pop parody. Their main influence in this area was American group The Four Preps, whose 1961 US Top 20 hit, 'More Money For You & Me', was the blueprint for the British group's success. The Barron Knights, who started life as a trio, were formed by Barron Anthony (Anthony Osmond) and featured vocalist Duke D'mond (Richard Palmer). They were regulars on both the British and German club circuit in the early 1960s, and appeared in *The Beatles Christmas Show* in 1963. After a couple of non-hits, 'Call Up The Groups' (based on the Four Preps 1962 release, 'The Big Draft'), took them to the higher reaches of the charts, alongside The Rolling Stones, The Searchers, Freddie & The Dreamers and The Bachelors, all of whom were parodied on the single by the Barron Knights. The group made serious records, but all their major successes came with pastiche parodies of other people's hits. An act that has never been short of well-paid cabaret work, they also scored with 'Pop Goes the Workers' in 1965, 'Merrie Gentle Pops' in 1966 and 'Under New Management' the following year. They also returned to the Top 10 in the late 1970s with the similarly styled 'Live In Trouble' and 'A Taste Of Aggro'.

BRITS GREATEST YEAR

The last three new British groups to reach the Top 20 in their homeland in 1964 were The Pretty Things, Wayne Fontana & The Mindbenders and The Rockin' Berries. By comparison, The Pretty Things made The Rolling Stones seem as straight-laced as The Stones had made The Beatles appear. Physically, The Pretty Things were way ahead of The Stones in both the unkempt and unattractive stakes, whilst their untutored and unrefined R&B made The Stones sound like professional musicians. If an outrageous appearance and an uninhibited British R&B sound had been the main criteria for mid-1960s success, then The Pretty Things would have had a list of hits as long as lead singer Phil May's hair. As it was, they were too over the top for the average record buyer, and they had to contend themselves with just a trio of successful British singles.

The Mindbenders (right) after the departure of Wayne Fontana and (opposite) The Rockin' Berries

1964
TOP SINGLES ARTISTS IN THE UK

1	**THE BEATLES**	PARLOPHONE *UK*
2	**THE BACHELORS**	DECCA *UK*
3	**THE SEARCHERS**	PYE *UK*
4	**ROY ORBISON**	LONDON AMERICAN *US*
5	**MANFRED MANN**	HMV *UK*
6	**THE ROLLING STONES**	DECCA *UK*
7	**CILLA BLACK**	PARLOPHONE *UK*
8	**THE HOLLIES**	PARLOPHONE *UK*
9	**JIM REEVES**	RCA *US*
10	**THE DAVE CLARK FIVE**	COLUMBIA *UK*
11	**DUSTY SPRINGFIELD**	PHILIPS *UK*
12	**CLIFF RICHARD**	COLUMBIA *UK*
13	**GENE PITNEY**	UA *US*
14	**THE SWINGING BLUE JEANS**	HMV *UK*
15	**ELVIS PRESLEY**	RCA *US*
16	**THE SUPREMES**	STATESIDE *US*
17	**THE KINKS**	PYE *UK*
18	**THE ANIMALS**	COLUMBIA *UK*
19	**THE FOUR PENNIES**	PHILIPS *UK*
20	**PETER & GORDON**	COLUMBIA *UK*

Manchester's Mindbenders were the only one of the last trio of new British hit groups to crack the US charts. The quartet, fronted by photogenic Wayne Fontana, scored an American No. 1 with the 'Game Of Love' and, after Fontana's departure, 'A Groovy Kind Of Love' almost repeated that feat. The success of Birmingham's Rockin' Berries was confined to the UK. The quintet's cover versions of 'He's In Town' (a mid-table hit in the USA for The Tokens) and 'Poor Man's Son' both climbed into the Top 10. Incidentally, the group were noted for their humorous stage act which included impressions, by lead singer Chris Lea, of performers such as Louis Armstrong, Gene Vincent, Cliff Richard, Billy Fury and Johnny Mathis.

Billboard described 1964 as 'undoubtedly the greatest year in the history of the British record industry', and statistics more than backed up this lofty statement. The amount of money spent on records in the UK skyrocketed up by 18% to a record $71.5 million. UK acts held the top spot in Britain for all but six weeks of the year, while in the States British artists reigned at the summit for 24 weeks (18 by The Beatles). In total, 15 British records were included in the year's Top 40 singles in America, and 10 UK artists were in the list of 1964's Top US Singles Artists. These most impressive figures were naturally well received in Great Britain. On the British down side though, American songsmiths wrote the UK's No. 1s for over half the year, while in the USA only The Beatles took an original composition to the top. It was also a fact that the style of music known as Merseybeat was fast becoming passé on both sides of the Atlantic, and many of the British acts, who had emerged so dramatically in 1963 and early 1964, already had their biggest hits behind them. As the year closed there was also a sneaking suspicion that America's love affair with all things British might be cooling off, and that 1965 could see the USA regaining much of the ground it had lost to the British invaders.

DAVE CLARK FIVE

Londoner Dave Clark formed his first group in 1958. By the time of their debut single 'Chaquita' in 1962, the quintet had shed its original singer Stan Saxon and consisted of Dave Clark (drums), Mike Smith (keyboards, lead vocal), Lenny Davidson (guitar), Denis Payton (saxophone) and Rick Huxley (guitar). They followed their Ember release with two equally unprofitable singles on Piccadilly, 'I Knew It All The Time' and 'First Love'. The distinctively dressed combo joined Columbia Records in 1963, and their third single on that label, 'Glad All Over', took them to the top of the British chart for the only time in their long and successful career. The group became transatlantic teen idols, amassing nine UK Top 20 singles and two Top 10 albums in the 1960s. Their main success, however, came on the other side of the Atlantic, where they were the second British beat group to

Dave Clark, bottom right, with his Five – (clockwise) Rick Huxley, Denis Payton, Lenny Davidson and Mike Smith

break down the barriers. Between 1964 and 1967, US record buyers held the photogenic fivesome in almost as high esteem as The Beatles. In total, six of their albums reached the Top 20, while two dozen of their singles hit the chart, 14 of which climbed into the Top 20. Surprisingly, several of their big US hits, which were a combination of originals and covers, failed to arouse much interest in their homeland. Even their 1965 revival of Bobby Day's 1958 B-side, 'Over And Over', which topped the American listings, came a UK chart cropper. Among Clark's catalogue of US chart entries were the self-composed 'Can't You See That She's Mine' and 'Because' in 1964, plus a rocking revival of Chris Kenner's 'I Like It Like That' a year later. The hugely popular group played cameo roles in several low budget pop films, and the title song from their own starring vehicle *Catch Us If You Can* (re-titled *Having A Wild Weekend* in the US) gave them their only transatlantic Top 10 entry in 1965. The quintet, who made a record dozen appearances on Ed Sullivan's American TV show, could not ring the musical changes as The Beatles did, and they finally ran out of steam Stateside in 1968. The Dave Clark Five then turned their full attention back to the UK, where they managed a few more reasonable sellers before the decade closed. The multi-platinum group disbanded in 1973. The shrewd Clark has since become a successful music business entrepreneur.

MANFRED MANN

Johannesburg-born keyboard player Manfred Mann (born Michael Lubowitz), who had attended the prestigious Juilliard School Of Music in New York, formed the jazz-based R&B band the Mann-Hugg Blues Brothers with drummer Mike Hugg in 1962. The other members of the hip looking quintet were Paul Jones (born Paul Pond) (vocals, harmonica), a youthful veteran of both skiffle and trad jazz bands, Mike Vickers (guitar), who had previously written arrangements for noted jazz musician Johnny Dankworth, and Dave Richmond (bass), whose place was soon relinquished to Tom McGuinness. After a name change (HMV Records insisted they chose a more commercial one), the credible crew released the bluesy self-penned instrumental 'Why Should We Not?', followed by the catchy 'Cock-A-Hoop'. Both narrowly missed the chart. Manfred Mann went on to become one of the most revered bands in Britain in the 1960s. They scored three Top 10 albums and three No. 1 singles; 'Do Wah Diddy Diddy' in 1964,' 'Pretty Flamingo' (first recorded by American Tommy Vann) in 1966 and 'Mighty Quinn' in 1968. The latter song was their third major hit penned by Bob Dylan, following 'If You Gotta Go, Go Now' and 'Just Like A Woman' (their first single on Fontana). Jones went solo in 1966, and simultaneously the band's current bass player, Jack Bruce, left to form Cream. Rod Stewart and Long John Baldry were among Jones' possible replacements, but the position went to Mike D'Abo (from The Band Of Angels). In 1969, the group evolved into Manfred Mann Chapter Three and in 1972 into the successful Manfred Mann's Earth Band. Jones had UK Top 10 entries with both 'High Time' and 'I've Been A Bad Bad Boy' in the mid-1960s, and is still a noted figure in the British entertainment field as singer, broadcaster and sometime actor.

Manfred Mann (left) made the transition from cellar clubs to showbiz glitter, as did heart throbs The Merseybeats (below)

Manfred Mann, one of the most durable performers of that decade, has recorded regularly since the Sixties and still retains a loyal, if not large, following.

THE MERSEYBEATS

In 1961 Tony Crane (vocals, lead guitar) and Billy Kinsley (vocal, bass) formed The Mavericks. This duo expanded to a quartet in 1962, when they adopted the name The Merseybeats. The group, which then included Aaron Williams (rhythm guitar) and John Banks (drums), decided to specialise in ballads, in order to stand out from most of the other artists in the Liverpool area. The snappily dressed act's debut single in 1963 was a revival of Ruby & The Romantics US No. 1, 'Our Day Will Come', on Oriole. It fell by the wayside, but their next release, Bacharach and David's atmospheric ballad 'It's Love That Really Counts', produced by Jack Baverstock on Fontana, reputedly sold over 100,000 (despite failing to make it into the *NME* Top 30). The Merseybeats, who never cracked the American chart, reached their commercial pinnacle in 1964 when three singles and an album entered the UK Top 20. In 1966 the group pruned down to the original duo, adopted a similarly pruned name, The Merseys, and returned briefly to the heights with 'Sorrow' (originally cut by US pop group The McCoys).

FOUR PENNIES

The Four Pennies were formed in 1963 in Blackburn, Lancashire, starting life as the Lionel Morton Four. They comprised Lionel Morton (Vocal, lead guitar), Fritz Fryer (lead guitar), Mike Wilsh (bass) and Alan Buck (drums). Morton had previously been a solo singer, Fryer and Wilsh had both been members of

Irish group Them, featuring Van Morrison, moved to London, where they were billed as 'Raving R&B'

	TITLE	ARTIST
1	I FEEL FINE	THE BEATLES
2	GLAD ALL OVER	THE DAVE CLARK FIVE
3	YOU'RE MY WORLD	CILLA BLACK
4	IT'S OVER	ROY ORBISON
5	A HARD DAY'S NIGHT	THE BEATLES
6	OH PRETTY WOMAN	ROY ORBISON
7	NEEDLES AND PINS	THE SEARCHERS
8	CAN'T BUY ME LOVE	THE BEATLES
9	DO WAH DIDDY DIDDY	MANFRED MANN
10	ANYONE WHO HAD A HEART	CILLA BLACK
11	HAVE I THE RIGHT?	THE HONEYCOMBS
12	I'M INTO SOMETHING GOOD	HERMAN'S HERMITS
13	LITTLE CHILDREN	BILLY J. KRAMER & THE DAKOTAS
14	BABY LOVE	THE SUPREMES
15	A WORLD WITHOUT LOVE	PETER & GORDON
16	IT'S ALL OVER NOW	THE ROLLING STONES
17	DIANE	THE BACHELORS
18	YOU REALLY GOT ME	THE KINKS
19	DON'T THROW YOUR LOVE AWAY	THE SEARCHERS
20	ALWAYS SOMETHING THERE TO REMIND ME	SANDIE SHAW

In June, for the first time in 18 months, an American single – 'It's Over' by Roy Orbison – topped the British charts

Lead guitarist Fritz Fryer fronting The Four Pennies

The Fables, while Buck had played with Joe Brown and Johnny Kidd. The group's first Philips Records release, 'Do You Want Me To', narrowly missed the chart, and it was the self-written 'Juliet', the intended B-side of their second single, 'Tell Me Girl', which made their name. Before 1964 ended, the group returned to the Top 30 with Fryer's composition, 'I Found Out The Hard Way', a revival of folk/blues legend Leadbelly's 'Black Girl' and Buffy Sainte-Marie's haunting ballad, 'Until It's Time For You To Go'. In 1966, when their appeal seemed to have evaporated, they decided it was time to go their separate ways. Morton, whose years spent in a cathedral choir were self-evident in his vocals, later recorded as a solo artist and for a while became a children's television personality (appearing on programmes like *Play Away*), while Fryer had some success as a record producer, working with numerous acts such as Motorhead. Incidentally, a new line-up of the group, this time simply called The Pennies, re-recorded 'Juliet' unsuccessfully in the mid 1970s.

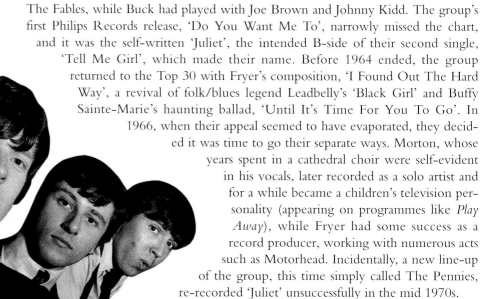

HERMAN'S HERMITS

This Manchester quintet, initially performing as Peter Novak & The Heartbeats, occupied a pivitol role in the Beat Boom. The members were Peter 'Herman' Noone (lead vocals), Derek Leckenby (guitar), Keith Hopwood (guitar), Karl Green (bass) and Barry Whitwam (drums). Occasionally though, session men such as Jimmy Page and John Paul Jones (both later of Led Zeppelin), were recruited to play on their records. Herman, whose nickname came from his supposed resemblance to Sherman in the *Rocky & Bullwinkle* cartoons, said the group's music 'was styled on the American surfing sound, which we all like.' Their first release on Columbia, 'I'm Into Something Good', was the biggest of their many British hits. Herman wanted it known that 'We didn't get this song from Earl-Jean's American hit version', explaining they had based their interpretation on composer Carole King's demo. From the outset, producer Mickie Most realised the American potential of the cute 16 year old singer with the passing resemblance to the late President John F. Kennedy. In 1965, Herman's Hermits were the most successful singles act in the USA, having Transatlantic Top 10 hits with revivals of 'Silhouettes', a major American hit for The Rays in 1957, and Sam Cooke's 'Wonderful World'. The highly touted group had three Top 5 albums there, sold out concerts from coast to coast, and regularly appeared in all the teen oriented magazines in the States. After The Beatles, they had the biggest 'teenybopper' following of all the British Invasion acts. Their biggest US successes came with revivals of Tom Courtenay's 1963 release, 'Mrs. Brown You've Got A Lovely Daughter' (which inspired several subsequent answer records), and the old music hall favourite, 'I'm Henry VIII I Am'. Surprisingly, both were thought to be 'too British' for consumption in Britain, which meant they were not released as singles in Britain. Herman's Hermits, who had no aversion to borrowing songs from other artists and indeed other eras, played cameo roles in several movies as well as starring in their own film, *Hold On*, in 1965. Many critics claim the arrival in 1967 on the American scene of another Manchester born actor/singer with a not dissimilar image, Davy Jones (of The Monkees), hastened the end of Hermania. Either way, the hits halted Stateside for Herman's Hermits in 1968, and two years later 'Lady Barbara' on Mickie Most's RAK label, became the accomplished act's last UK chart entry. After the group split in 1970, Noone recorded as a soloist with minimal success, and both he and The Hermits have, every so often, done the nostalgia circuit. One of the best examples was their 1986 US tour with the aforementioned Davy Jones and The Monkees. Noone is now a well known VJ in the United States, having hosted the successful music magazine, *My Generation*, as well as the *Billboard* Video Awards Show in 1992. Perhaps more than any other British group, Herman's Hermits used their accents to great advantage – to paraphrase their biggest hit, 'groups like them were really something rare!'

ANIMALS

In 1962, Tyne & Wear group The Alan Price Trio, which comprised Price (keyboards), Bryan 'Chas' Chandler (bass) and John Steel (drums), recruited gruff voiced ex-Pagans' singer Eric Burdon (vocals) and Wild Cats guitarist Hilton Valentine. The R&B quintet performed for a while as the Alan Price Combo, before being re-christened The Animals. After honing their act at the Star Club in Hamburg in 1963, the distinctive group, with its short–haired yet streetwise image, headed for London, where they were soon playing regularly at trendy clubs like *The Scene*. Former singer turned producer Mickie Most spotted their potential and persuaded Columbia Records to let him produce them. Their first release was an old blues song which Bob Dylan had recorded on his eponymous debut album as 'Baby Let Me Follow You Down'. The Animals' adaptation entitled 'Baby Let Me

In September American country & Western singer Jim Reeves had a record eight LPs in the UK Album Top 20

Peter Noone (centre) was a teen actor whose parts had included TV's *Coronation Street* before he became Herman of the Hermits

Take You Home' became the first of a dozen UK Top 20 hits for the consistently enjoyable group. The follow-up, the unforgettable organ-led 'House Of The Rising Sun', followed a similar pattern, being an old blues song which Dylan had included on his first LP. The group ignored pleas that the record was too long at four and a half minutes (the average single then being two minutes shorter!); BBC radio told them: 'Kids would prefer to hear two records by different artists than one long one', but the quintet's decision proved correct, and the record, which had only taken them 20 minutes to record, went on to top the chart on both sides of the Atlantic. It was voted Best Record of 1964 in the UK, and elevated the group to superstar status. Among their ten American Top 20 hits were such transatlantic successes as 'Don't Let Me Be Misunderstood' (originally a hit by Nina Simone), 'We've Got To Get Out Of This Place' (written by the top US team of Barry Mann & Cynthia Weil for the Righteous Brothers) and 'Don't Bring Me Down' (composed by Gerry Goffin & Carole King). Unlike many of the British groups of the era, The Animals also sold vast quantities of albums, with five of their LPs gracing the UK Top 20 and three reaching the equivalent American listing. Price (who hated flying) was the first member to leave, and by mid-1966, Eric Burdon fronted a completely new line-up of Animals. It was this new team which scored the group's final transatlantic Top 10 hit, the self-composed 'San Franciscan Nights', in 1967. Both Eric Burdon and Alan Price had later recording success outside The Animals, while Chas Chandler became a top manager handling such acts as Jimi Hendrix and Slade. The original quintet has sporadically re-united to record or play selected dates, and every decade the haunting 'House Of The Rising Sun' rises up the British chart again.

Charismatic front men, The Animals' Eric Burdon (above) and Ray Davies of The Kinks

THE KINKS

The Kinks retained their transatlantic popularity long after most Beat Boom bands had disappeared without trace. In fact the group were still in operation, and still in demand, in the early 1990s with founder members (and brothers) Ray & Dave Davies fronting the otherwise much changed combo. Ex-art school student Ray and his brother had formed the group in North London in late 1963 with Peter Quaife (bass) and Mick Avory (drums). Prior to this singer/guitarist/songwriter Ray had played in both the Dave Hunt Band and in brother Dave's group, The Ravens. The Kinks signed with Pye in early 1964 and their riff-laden third single, 'You Really Got Me', topped the UK chart, and reached the US Top 10. The follow-up, 'All Day And All Of The Night' was a transatlantic Top 3 hit, and their next single,' Tired Of Waiting For You', became their second UK No. 1 and third US Top 10 entry. Despite continued British success The Kinks did not return to the American Top 10 during the 1960s, possibly because they were barred from performing there for several years after abandoning an American tour at short notice. This may also have been part of the reason for Ray Davies' emergence as the quintessential English songwriter, whose timeless mid-1960s classics include 'Dedicated Follower of Fashion' (a tongue-in-cheek comment on the Carnaby Street and whole Swinging London scen), the lusciously lazy lament 'Sunny Afternoon' (their third British chart topper), the picturesque 'Waterloo Sunset' (which had started life as 'Liverpool Sunset') and 'Autumn Almanac'. In total, The Kinks had 17 British and seven US Top 20 singles, and also sold vast quantities albums, by the end of the 1960s putting six LPs into the UK Top 20, and thr

the US Top 40. The group continued to add to their transatlantic hit tally in the 1970s and 1980s, and have remained a popular act and a well-used source of material throughout the rock era. It came as no surprise when they became the fourth British group to be inducted into the Rock'n'Roll Hall Of Fame, after The Beatles, The Rolling Stones and The Who.

PRETTY THINGS

A no-holds-barred R&B quintet formed in Dartford, Kent, and named after a Bo Diddley song, the 'Fings' were fronted by vocalist Phil May, who, it was claimed, had the longest hair (on a man) in Britain. The rest of the group were Dick Taylor (guitar), who had played with Mick Jagger and Keith Richards in Little Boy Blue & The Blue Boys (an embryonic Rolling Stones), Brian Pendleton (rhythm guitar), John Stax (bass) and Viv Prince (drums), an ex-member of one-time chart act Carter-Lewis & The Southerners. Not surprisingly, this ill-groomed combo were often compared to the Stones, although their brand of R&B had an even more abandoned, almost destructive, attitude and approach; if there was such a thing as an R&B punk band, this was it. The Pretty Things first single on Fontana, 'Rosalyn' (a close relative of New Orleans R&B singer Benny Spellman's 'Fortune Teller'), attracted a lot of attention but narrowly missed the chart. Nonetheless, before Prince left in late 1965, the group had amassed a Top 10 album and three

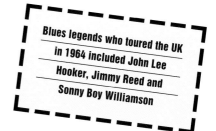

Successful UK tours were made by US rock veterans Jerry Lee Lewis, Little Richard, Bill Haley, Chuck Berry and Carl Perkins

The notorious 'Pretties' with (left to right) Stax, Taylor, Prince, Pendleton and May

Top 20 singles; 'Don't Bring Me Down', their own song 'Honey I Need', plus a version of Solomon Burke's US R&B hit, 'Cry To Me'. In America, despite an appearance on the prestigious *Shindig* television programme, the unmistakable group garnered few sales. Nonetheless, they did attract some US notoriety when several stations banned 'Don't Bring Me Down' because of the line 'I laid her on the ground.' In 1968, when their long-haired hippy image had become almost the norm, they released their highly regarded concept album, *S.F. Sorrow*, which many consider to have been the inspiration for The Who's *Tommy*. In 1973, David

Blues legends who toured the UK in 1964 included John Lee Hooker, Jimmy Reed and Sonny Boy Williamson

1964 TOP SINGLES IN THE US

	TITLE	ARTIST
1	I WANT TO HOLD YOUR HAND	THE BEATLES
2	THERE I'VE SAID IT AGAIN	BOBBY VINTON
3	BABY LOVE	THE SUPREMES
4	CAN'T BUY ME LOVE	THE BEATLES
5	HELLO, DOLLY!	LOUIS ARMSTRONG
6	SHE LOVES YOU	THE BEATLES
7	OH PRETTY WOMAN	ROY ORBISON
8	HOUSE OF THE RISING SUN	THE ANIMALS
9	COME SEE ABOUT ME	THE SUPREMES
10	CHAPEL OF LOVE	THE DIXIE CUPS
11	I GET AROUND	THE BEACH BOYS
12	WHERE DID OUR LOVE GO	THE SUPREMES
13	I FEEL FINE	THE BEATLES
14	DO WAH DIDDY DIDDY	MANFRED MANN
15	MY GUY	MARY WELLS
16	A HARD DAY'S NIGHT	THE BEATLES
17	RAG DOLL	THE FOUR SEASONS
18	MR. LONELY	BOBBY VINTON
19	EVERYBODY LOVES SOMEBODY	DEAN MARTIN
20	A WORLD WITHOUT LOVE	PETER & GORDON

The Rockin' Berries (opposite) were typical of the well-groomed groups who never grew out of their Beat Boom suits

Bowie recorded two of their hits on his Pin Ups album, and in 1974, this controversial combo, with its ever-changing personnel, signed to Led Zeppelin's Swan Song label. The Pretty Things, who finally made their debut on the US chart in 1975, were still recording in the 1990s.

WAYNE FONTANA & THE MINDBENDERS

Manchester born Wayne Fontana (real name Glynn Ellis) started like many other British artists of the era in a school skiffle group (The Velfins). In 1961 he formed The Jets, a group that evolved into The Mindbenders (named after a Dirk Bogarde film). The line-up comprised Eric Stewart (guitar), Bob Lang (bass) and Ric Rothwell (drums). Their first release, which coupled a revival of Fats Domino's 'Hello Josephine' with an update of Bo Diddley's 'Road Runner', was a minor hit, as was their version of Ben E. King's 'Stop Look and Listen'. After this modest start, the quartet finally made their commercial breakthrough with their fifth Jack Baverstock produced single on Fontana, 'Um, Um, Um, Um, Um, Um' (a cover of Major Lance's biggest US hit), which only just missed the top of the British chart. Their follow-up, a Clint Ballard Jr. composition, 'Game of Love', fared even better, taking the quartet to the top of the American charts in 1965 and returning

them to the UK Top 3. Ballard then wrote 'I'm Alive' especially for them, but it was rejected as 'rubbish' – it later gave The Hollies their first No. 1. In October 1965, after a couple of less successful singles, the group and its vocalist went their separate ways. Both acts racked up two more UK Top 20 hits, with the group getting the lion's share of sales. Photogenic, tambourine-touting Fontana, who had been voted 'Best New Singer Of 1965' in the UK, scored with 'Come On Home', written by reggae star Jackie Edwards, and 'Pamela Pamela' composed by Graham Gouldman. The Mindbenders hit in 1966 with two Toni Wine & Carole Bayer compostions, 'A Groovy Kind Of Love' (previously recorded by Patti Labelle & The Bluebelles) and 'Ashes To Ashes', with the former giving them a Transatlantic Top 3 entry (a 1988 revival by Phil Collins went to No. 1 on both sides of the Atlantic). In 1968, songwriter Graham Gouldman joined The Mindbenders, who soon afterwards evolved into Hotlegs and then into the ultra-successful 10cc. From time to time, Fontana reappears on the cabaret and nostalgia circuit with a new line up of Mindbenders.

ROCKIN' BERRIES

This Birmingham quintet, formed in 1961, consisted of Chris Lea (lead singer), Geoff Turton (guitar, falsetto vocals), Chuck Botfield (guitar), Terry Bond (drums) and Roy Austin (bass). Like many of their contemporaries, they worked in Germany in the early 1960s and signed to Decca in 1963. The group's first two releases were 'Wah Wah Wah Woo' and a critically applauded, though only moderately popular, version of James Ray's 'Itty Bitty Pieces'. Piccadilly Records recruited the Rockin' Berries in 1964, and their second release for the label, a falsetto-fronted adaptation of the Carole King song, 'He's In Town', took them into the UK Top 5. In 1965, 'Poor Man's Son', which featured Lea and Turton on a carefully cloned cover of The Reflections US hit, gave them their second and last major chart success. The group's indulgence with comedy and impressions on stage is quoted both as a reason for their relatively short chart life, and as an explanation for their long club and cabaret career. When Turton went solo in 1969, his single, 'Baby Take Me In Your Arms' (released under the name Jefferson), reached the Top 40 on both sides of the Atlantic.

1964
TOP SINGLES ARTISTS IN THE US

1	**THE BEATLES**	CAPITOL *UK*
2	**THE DAVE CLARK FIVE**	EPIC *UK*
3	**THE SUPREMES**	MOTOWN *US*
4	**THE FOUR SEASONS**	VEE JAY *US*
5	**BOBBY VINTON**	EPIC *US*
6	**THE BEACH BOYS**	CAPITOL *US*
7	**JAN & DEAN**	LIBERTY *US*
8	**ROY ORBISON**	MONUMENT *US*
9	**THE SHANGRI-LAS**	RED BIRD *US*
10	**JOHNNY RIVERS**	IMPERIAL *US*
11	**DEAN MARTIN**	REPRISE *US*
12	**PETER & GORDON**	CAPITOL *UK*
13	**LESLEY GORE**	MERCURY *US*
14	**MARY WELLS**	MOTOWN *US*
15	**THE DIXIE CUPS**	RED BIRD *US*
16	**GERRY & THE PACEMAKERS**	LAURIE *UK*
17	**THE IMPRESSIONS**	ABC PARAMOUNT *US*
18	**MARTHA & THE VANDELLAS**	GORDY *US*
19	**DIONNE WARWICK**	SCEPTER *US*
20	**BETTY EVERETT**	VEE JAY *US*

Mop tops and mutineers

THE BEATLES AND THE 'STONES

The Beatles: John Lennon (vocals, rhythm guitar), Paul McCartney (vocals, bass), George Harrison (vocals, lead guitar), Ringo Starr (vocals, drums)

The Beatles are the most important and influential group of the rock era, and there is a good chance that without them there would have been no Beat Boom or British Invasion.

Since their story is arguably the best known in rock, this book will try to avoid too much repetition by simply taking a chronological look at some interesting and hopefully less documented items from their early days.

The Kinks leader, Ray Davies, thought 'The Beatles got their unique sound by trying to copy Little Richard.' Be that as it may, on their first major tour in October 1962, the group supported their admitted hero, Little Richard, and the last song they ever performed live was the American rocker's hit, 'Long Tall Sally'. In December 1962, a month before 'Please Please Me' was released, the quartet played 13 nights at the Star Club, Hamburg, supporting American instrumental rock band, Johnny & The Hurricanes. Incidentally, when The Beatles returned to Hamburg in 1966, they were given an eight-car motorcade.

The Beatles toured with American Chris Montez in March, and his collar-less jackets so intrigued them that they had similar stage suits made. 'Please Please Me' was rush released in America in Spring 1963, but despite reasonable air play and passable sales, it failed to crack the Top 100. Many UK record buyers who bought

The Mop Tops arrive complete with BEAtles bags specially supplied by the UK airline BEA

the album, Please Please Me, solely because of its title track, were pleasantly surprised by the standard of songs and the fact that The Beatles, unlike other groups, possessed two impressive lead vocalists. However, a poll taken in Summer 1963, among teenage children of American Air Force personnel in Britain, showed that most felt The Beatles would never happen in their homeland. In the United States,

the group's first album, which was re-titled Introducing The Beatles, was unsuccessfully released in the July of 1963. Their August release, 'She Loves You', sold over 1.5 million in Britain in record time, and that month they also played their 274th and last show at the Cavern Club. The word 'Beatlemania' was coined in late 1963, about the time they appeared live on British TVs' most successful show, *Sunday Night At The London Palladium*. Several music critics thought the show might harm their career, since it showed that, when singing live and not drowned by screams, Paul possessed a relatively weak voice. The Fabulous

"Beatlemania bug has arrived in epidemic proportions and is giving trade a solid bite"

Billboard

The Beatles take in the sights from New York's Central Park, February 1964

Four also played for the Queen Mother and Princess Margaret at the *Royal Variety Show* in November - it was the seal of approval from the Establishment. With British advance orders of almost a million, 'I Want To Hold Your Hand' was one of five Beatles recordings in the Top 20 singles chart as the year closed (two of them were actually EPs and one an album!). Their composition 'I Wanna Be Your Man' was also in the chart, performed by The Rolling Stones.

AMERICA FLIPS ITS WIG

In early January, 1964, *NME* announced that there would be a massive Stateside campaign behind The Beatles, and McCartney said 'It would knock us out to go over there and make good'. The US trade paper, *Cash Box*, called 'I Want To Hold Your Hand' 'an infectious twist-like thumper that could spread like wildfire here.' *Billboard* reported in late January 1964, 'The Beatlemania bug has arrived in

Beatle Wigs, 1964 vintage, now fetch three-figure prices in rock memorabilia sales all over the world

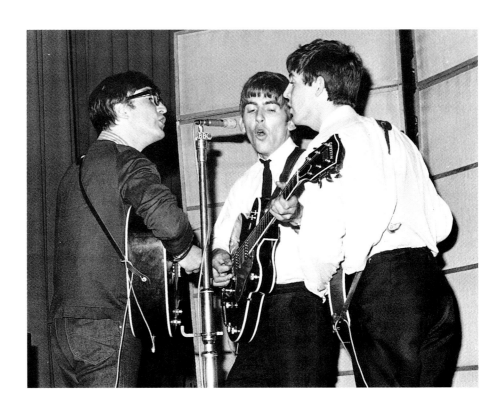

The Beatles at the Beeb, making one of many live appearances on British radio during 1963

American female vocal trio The Ronettes supported both The 'Stones and Beatles on tour in 1964

epidemic proportions and is giving trade a solid bite.' While the Mop Tops' label, Capitol, boasted about the success of their $50,000 nation-wide promotional campaign, law suits flew between them and other labels over the rights to earlier Beatles tracks that Capitol had previously rejected - proof of the old music biz proverb, 'where there's a hit there's a writ'. Top American TV show host, Ed Sullivan, who had initially been less than convinced of the group's potential, was very surprised when the act he booked for less than $3,000 attracted a record 73 million viewers. Despite these figures, reviews of their performance were 'mild'. The US correspondent for *NME* wrote 'Except for their visual uniqueness, The Beatles are a run of the mill rock'n'roll attraction,' and concluded 'the musical reason for all the excitement escapes me.' Also that month *Billboard*, for the first time in its long history, ran a photo of an act as part of its front page logo, to emphasise their lead story 'US rocks & reels from Beatles invasion.' Inside the magazine, other articles informed readers of the situation nation-wide: 'Chicago flips its wig - Beatles and otherwise,' 'New York City is crawling with Beatlemania' and 'Beatle binge in L.A.'

Among the supporting acts on The Beatles' first American show in February were The Chiffons (whose biggest hit, 'He's So Fine', was proved to have influenced George Harrison when he wrote 'My Sweet Lord') and Tommy Roe, whom they had supported in the UK in 1963. By the end of February, the foursome had the top two albums in America, an amazing feat which they repeated twice more that year. In March, Vee Jay Records released an album titled Jolly What! (now worth over $250), which coupled tracks by The Beatles and Frank Ifield! That same month, *Billboard* introduced a new award to commemorate the group having the top three singles. By the time it was ready for presentation, The Beatles occupied the top five positions, and a new trophy was commissioned. The magazine's headlines screamed 'Nobody loves The Beatles, 'cept mother, Capitol etc', and explained that The Beatles were bad for the US music business, as the only products people wanted seemed to be theirs. While the quartet were smashing many records set earlier by Elvis, Presley's label RCA, not to be out-done, announced that his total sales were now over 100,000,000. Also in March, 'Can't Buy Me Love' logged unprecedented advance orders on both sides of the Atlantic - orders in Britain were over a million, and in the States more than double that figure. During the two months following their US chart debut, they collected a staggering six gold singles, and the Meet The Beatles album (the first LP by a rock group to top the US chart) sold nearly four million copies.

UNEQUALLED RECORDS

April found them nabbing the first six slots on the Australian chart and the first nine in Canada. *Billboard*, whose top hundred then included an unprecedented 13 Beatles' tracks, announced, 'The American Chart Crawls with Beatles' and explained 'everyone is tired of The Beatles except the listening and buying public.' By May, the group had three of the Top 4 albums in the USA. In June they attracted a record 250,000 to a show in Melbourne, Australia, and a month later a similar sized crowd packed their route to the Liverpool city centre, when they were honoured by their hometown. On the Mop Tops' Autumn US tour, the supporting acts included Bill Black, the bass player who had backed Elvis on his first tours.

In 1964, The Beatles became the first act to gross over $1 million from a tour, and it was reported that their merchandising grossed $50 million. So great was their impact in the USA that even the then staid and anti-rock Grammy awards committee, acknowledged them as Best New Act and 'A Hard Day's Night' as Best Group Recording. Meanwhile back in Britain, they became the first rockers to receive MBEs from Queen Elizabeth - a fact that upset many other holders of that honour.

It's common knowledge that every record the group released was a huge hit. In Britain, they have had a record 12 No. 1 albums, spent 163 weeks at the top (three times more than their nearest rival),

"Except for their visual uniqueness, The Beatles are a run of the mill rock'n'roll attraction, the musical reason for all the excitement escapes me."

NME

Before the ballyhoo Stateside, The Beatles in 1963 in an appearance on British television

and their four-million-selling Sergeant Pepper's Lonely Hearts Club Band is the all-time top selling LP. In America, they released a record 15 chart-topping albums, and earned an unequalled 16 platinum and six quintuple platinum LPs. Their transatlantic singles track record is no less impressive. The group notched up 17 British and 20 American No. 1s, and on top of this they accumulated 24 con-secutive UK Top 10 singles (including 12 consecutive No. 1s) and 15 consecutive US Top 5 singles (including six consecutive No. 1s). To these stunning statistics can be added the fact that Lennon & McCartney's 'Yesterday' has become the most performed pop song ever in America, with nearly six million radio plays, and that in 1964 The Beatles scored a record 11 US Top 10 singles in one calendar year. The group also spent not only the most weeks at the top of the UK singles chart, but also the most at the top of the UK and US album charts. Impressive as these figures are, it is the timeless quality of the music behind these statistics that made The Beatles so special. It was the consistency and freshness of their work that made them so successful in the Sixties, and which continues to captivate generation after generation.

An injured police woman can be seen being hauled onto the stage during a 'Stones 'riot' at Belle View, Manchester, in Summer '64

'Stones Vocalist Mick Jagger was voted Best New Male Singer in the 1964 NME Annual Readers Poll

The Rolling Stones: Mick Jagger (vocal), Keith Richards (rhythm guitar), Brian Jones (lead guitar), Bill Wyman (bass), Charlie Watts (drums).

The early Rolling Stones would have been amazed and possibly even insulted to know that one day they would be called The World's Greatest Rock'n'Roll Band. In those formative years, they did not consider themselves a rock act; rhythm and blues was their business. They felt more of an affinity with black R&B performers like Chuck Berry and Muddy Waters than they did with rock stars like Elvis Presley and Cliff Richard.

It is also easy to forget that the group, regarded by many as the epitome of self-reliant rock acts, were initially afraid that releasing one of their own songs as an A-side could harm their career. If we believe that unlike most recording acts in pre-Beat Boom Britain, The 'Stones had some freedom of choice when it came to recording, it is surprising they did not take more advantage of this situation to show how original and unique they were - as The Beatles did. Perhaps the fact that they genuinely felt that only Americans could write good R&B accounts for their lack of self confidence until they had the security of two UK No.1s behind them. Even then, the first Jagger-Richard song to chart by The Rolling Stones in Britain, the US-recorded 'The Last Time', owed a little to R&B/gospel act The Staples Singers' 'Maybe The Last Time'.

There is no question, however, that the group were always exciting on stage and that a good deal of their appeal can be credited to lead vocalist Jagger, a charismatic performer who owes much to his R&B and soul icons. The Beatles, and most other Northern groups, may initially have relied on songs and arrangements cribbed from their favourite American R&B acts, but The 'Stones, like many earlier British pop stars, went further by apeing the accents of their musical idols, with middle class Southerner Jagger trying his best to sound like a black American.

If proof were ever needed that a 'bad boy' image helps to sell records, one need look no further than The 'Stones. At the outset, they were not sold to the public as rebels, but this image, with help from manager Andrew Loog Oldham, evolved very quickly. Oldham knew there was always room for rebellion in rock, and when the general public accepted the one-time anti-establishment Beatles, he realised there was a niche for a new and even more outrageous band of 'baddies'. It was an image that originally was slightly at odds with the truth, and initially group members may have felt like actors playing a part. Nonetheless, they relished their roles and to all intents and purposes soon became the archetypal rock'n'roll rebels that the public perceived them to be.

BEATLE CRUSHERS?

The 'Stones were not instantly successful Stateside. After all, in May 1964, when their US debut, 'Not Fade Away', was released, Americans were only just getting accustomed to the look and sound of The Beatles, who in comparison looked like short-haired, well dressed 'All-American boys'. Many US parents were still not over enamoured by The Beatles, and none, surely, would have selected The Rolling Stones, with their obvious lack of respect for the establishment, as ideal idols or role models for their offspring.

In June 1964, *Billboard* carried a full page advert simply stating in large red print 'Watch the Rolling Stones crush The Beatles', and carrying the footnote 'this space has been given, in the public interest, by an advertiser, who wishes to remain anonymous'. Later that month the quintet toured the USA for the first time - ticket sales were disappointing, and far from crushing the Mop Tops, The Rolling Stones went home a little crushed and crestfallen themselves. However, by October, 1964, US pop record buyers had also warmed to Anglicised-American R&B, and the group had the first of their 30 Top 20 singles, 'Time Is On My Side' (first recorded by Irma Thomas). Also in October, they headlined the all-star TAMI (Teen-Age Music International) show, and had to follow one of their idols, James Brown, on stage. Jagger admitted 'We tried unsuccessfully for two days to change the bill around - I mean you can't follow an act like that.' As Wyman commented, 'Brown does the most incredible dancing during his act, like Mick but only 20 times faster.' In the end, the group decided to delay their entrance by 45 minutes to allow the crowd to cool down after Brown's amazing stage show. As nimble, energetic and exciting as Jagger is, he knew he would look leaden-footed compared to Brown.

Few people then would have prophesised that three decades later The 'Stones would still be considered rebellious and newsworthy, or how much success they would achieve. Since 1963, they have amassed a record 34 gold albums, half of which have also gone platinum. Thus far, the group have been responsible for 29 British and 30 US Top 10 LPs, including nine UK and US No. 1s. In the UK, the quintet also released 19 consecutive Top 10 singles, eight of which reached No. 1 (five in succession), whilst in the US, eight of their 23 Top 10 singles to date have been chart toppers.

The Rolling Stones, who started out basically as rhythm and blues imitators, ended up being probably the most imitated band in the world. It's mind-boggling to realise that the same act which played to half empty houses in minor venues on its first Stateside tour grossed a record-breaking $100 million from an American tour a quarter of a century later.

> The 'Stones were the first UK Beat Boom group to record in the 'States, cutting 'It's All Over Now' at Chess Records, Chicago

Charlie Watts, Mick Jagger and Keith Richards lighting up

Keep on running

The Moody Blues (above) and Herman's Hermits – here in 'city gent' outfits that were sure to please the American media – were among the success stories of '65

Worries over whether Britain's beat troops could hold their ground in the US in 1965 proved unfounded. More artists from the UK advanced towards the top of the American chart than in any other Beat Boom year. Despite slipping in popularity in their homeland, The Dave Clark Five remained among America's Top 10 singles acts of the year, and after a slow Stateside start, The Rolling Stones joined them in the front line. The success story of 1965, however, was Herman's Hermits who replaced The Beatles as the top singles act. Incidentally, these four groups were also the only artists from Britain to reach the US Top 10 album chart during that eventful year.

There were fewer new UK acts that made the best sellers on both sides of the Atlantic in 1965, but these included some of the biggest selling artists of the whole rock era. The first group to make their British Top 20 chart debut that year was The Moody Blues. Like many other British acts of the Beat Boom era this Birmingham band initially relied totally on US R&B material for their singles. Their first release, 'Steal You Heart Away', was written and originally performed by Bobby Parker, while 'Go Now', which topped the UK chart and reached the US Top 10, was first released by Bessie Banks, the wife of its composer Larry Banks. The group followed their million selling hit with yet another cover, 'I Don't Want To Go On Without You', previously recorded by The Drifters (as a tribute to their late lead singer Rudy Lewis). The Moody Blues were always an

There were good press write-ups for The Little Ravens, a group featuring 15 year-old Peter Frampton

March 1965, and Them, fronted by Van Morrison, appear on the UK's top-rated TV pop show *Ready Steady Go!*

above average group, a fact that became more obvious after a couple of personnel changes and the injection of their own original material. The group, who have sold over 50 million records world-wide, now more than deserve their own chapter in the history of rock.

BELFAST TO BIRMINGHAM

The next group to break through were Belfast boys Them, a raw R&B crew fronted by powerhouse vocalist Van Morrison. They first came to the public's attention with their second single, 'Baby Please Don't Go', a blues-based R&B stomper which reached the Top 10, thanks, in part, to its use as a theme song for TV's *Ready Steady Go*. Their follow-up, 'Here Comes The Night', almost hit the top and a bright future seemed certain. Nevertheless, internal problems led to personnel changes and within a year their sullen and soulful singer had left Them. The group continued to record without Morrison, but without success, and after a brief lay-off, Morrison returned as a solo artist. He went on to become (and still remains) one of the best respected singer/songwriters of the rock age.

There was a wide sweep of styles present in the British charts in 1965, with music ranging from Them's unruly R&B to the smooth close harmony falsetto sound of The Ivy League. The latter act comprised Birmingham boys John Carter (born John Shakespeare) Ken Lewis (born James Hawker) plus soprano Perry Ford (born Bryan Pugh). Carter and Lewis were no strangers to the music business, having written hits for Mike Sarne, Brenda Lee and their own group Carter Lewis & The Southerners (which had included Jimmy Page). The trio were much in demand as session singers before becoming The Ivy League and signing to Piccadilly Records in 1964. Their second single under that name, 'Funny How Love Can Be', took them into the UK Top 10. The follow-up, 'That's Why I'm Crying', reached the Top 20, while another of their compositions, 'Tossing And Turning', made the UK Top 3 and the American Top 100 in the summer of 1965. Something the trio's hits had in common was that they were all tearful tales. Ford explained, 'People compare us to The Beach Boys, but they sing about dancing on beaches and we prefer sadder things. We always write sad lyrics and sing sad harmonies as our voices blend better that way. We can't be jolly like Herman's Hermits, because we don't feel it.' In September 1965 a planned US promotion

David Bowie's group The Mannish Boys (named after a Muddy Waters song) released a revival of Bobby Bland's 'I Pity The Fool' on Parlophone

71

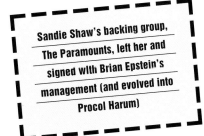

Sandie Shaw's backing group, The Paramounts, left her and signed with Brian Epstein's management (and evolved into Procol Harum)

Like their name suggested, the neatly turned out and smooth-sounding Ivy League

"People compare us to The Beach Boys, but they sing about dancing on beaches and we prefer sadder things. We can't be jolly like Herman's Hermits, because we don't feel it. "

The Ivy League's Perry Ford

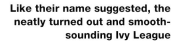

Marc Bolan released his first single, 'The Wizard', on Decca

trip had to be cancelled at the last minute when the American immigration people deemed them 'not unique' and refused them the necessary visa. Carter and Lewis pulled out of the act in 1966, and before the decade was over they had amassed between them an enviable number of hits as both writers and performers (under various noms-de-disque). Among the members' best known compositions were the Top 10 US entries 'Can't You Hear My Heartbeat' and 'Listen People' (both recorded by Herman's Hermits) and 'Little Bit O' Soul' (Music Explosion). There was also the transatlantic surf-styled smash 'Beach Baby' (by First Class), the major British successes, 'Semi-Detached Suburban Mr. Jones' (a Manfred Mann hit), 'Knock Knock Who's There' (Mary Hopkin), 'Peek-A-Boo' (The New Vaudeville Band) and the flower-power bandwagoner 'Let's Go To San Francisco' (Flowerpot Men).

OWN MATERIAL

Another new British outfit writing their own material was Hertfordshire pop sextet Unit Four Plus Two. Fronted by Tommy Moeller, they started as a modern folk act, simply known as Unit Four. After adding a two-man rhythm section, they naturally became Unit Four Plus Two. The sextet, who combined folk, pop and MOR, signed to Decca in 1964. Their first two releases, a cover of 'Greenfields' and the folky 'Sorrow and Pain', failed to click, but their third single, 'Concrete And Clay', quickly shot them to the top of the UK chart. Moeller wrote the song with an earlier Unit Four member Brian Parker (who found a measure of fame playing the guitar in The Hunters - a group that once backed another local lad, Cliff Richard). 'Concrete And Clay' possessed magic - it may have been the prominent use of a cowbell or the single's hypnotic Latin feel, but whatever the reason, it was one of the best-crafted pop records of the 1960s. A cash-in cover from US singer Eddie Rambeau hampered the single's progress in

America, and the result was sales were split, with both versions reaching the Top 40. This sextet, whose choice of songs was far more original than most British acts of the era, did manage a further four Top 30 entries, but none came anywhere close to equalling the success of their No. 1 record. For a short while noted song-writer and musician Russ Ballard joined the group, leaving before they folded in 1969. 'Concrete And Clay' returned to the UK Top 20 in 1976 in the hands of American singer/pianist Randy Edelman.

"We thought the British impact in the States was lessening. Now look at it - it's fantastic, incredible and staggering "

Freddie Garrity

MANCHESTER MANIA

By spring, 1965, America was starting to lose a little interest in groups from Liverpool, but this did not affect the quantity of British discs on the US chart, as Manchester-mania was mounting on the other side of the Atlantic. Herman's Hermits spearheaded the Mancunian invasion force, with Freddie & The Dreamers and Wayne Fontana & The Mindbenders close behind. In March, Herman's Hermits made their Top 10 debut with The Ivy League's bouncy composition 'Can't You Hear My Heartbeat'. At the same time, Americans finally fell for the madcap Freddie & The Dreamers, after seeing them perform on TV on *Hullaballoo* and *Shindig*. Within four weeks, they had four singles in the Top 100 including 'I'm Telling You Now' which stood at No. 1. 'Game Of Love' by Wayne Fontana & The Mindbenders followed it to the top, and this in turn was

'Concrete And Clay' stars Unit Four (minus Two!) get some new shoes beneath their feet

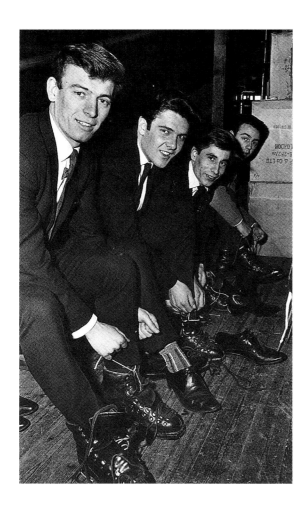

replaced by one of the fastest sellers in history - Herman's Hermits revival of the novelty, 'Mrs Brown You've Got A Lovely Daughter'. This trio of Manchester marvels took the tally of British No. 1s in America to 14 in as many months. Freddie (Garrity) exclaimed 'We thought the British impact in the States was lessening. Now look at it - it's fantastic, incredible and staggering.' Fontana was understandably a little less enthusiastic, as he was one of the acts having trouble getting the correct US visa. He may have had the nation's No. 1 record, but according to the American immigration authorities he was not well known enough to merit a full work permit. Herman (Peter Noone), who in June had three singles on the US Top 20, was delighted not only by his reception in the USA, but also because 'Americans are going mad for everything British.'

The highspot of the Swinging Sixties for UK acts in America came on May 8, when the US Top 10 contained a record nine British-recorded tracks: Herman's Hermits (who had two entries), The Beatles, Wayne Fontana & The Mindbenders, Freddie & The Dreamers, The Seekers (an Australian group who played a major role in the acceptance of folk-oriented music in the UK), The Rolling Stones, Petula Clark and Sounds Orchestral who each had one. The only act flying the stars and stripes that week was comedian Jerry Lewis' son Gary Lewis & The Playboys, a West Coast combo who inspired comparison with some of their British counterparts. For the record, seven days later American singles recaptured four slots.

"When I'm thirty I'm going to kill myself,

'cos I don't ever want to get old"

Pete Townshend

David Essex's version of
Solomon Burke's 'Can't Nobody
Love You' was released

MY GENERATION

Meanwhile, back in Britain The Who and The Yardbirds, two of the most important and influential acts of the rock era, were taking their first steps up the British chart. The Who were a revelation. Initially, they personified the early 1960s British mod, setting almost as many fashion trends as musical ones. If anything they were a notch more rebellious than The Rolling Stones, and at first their choice of material and indeed their style, was more original. The Who seemed hell-bent on breaking all the rules of pop music; delighting in destroying

Angry Mods The Who (right) called their act 'auto-destructive art' when leader Townshend took it out on his guitar (above)

The Clayton Squares (including this book's editor Mike Evans) released their first single

their instruments on stage and in creating ear-shattering feedback. They gave the appearance of being able to do exactly what they wanted, when they wanted and epitomised everything many of their generation would have liked to be. The group had their first three British hits in 1965; 'I Can't Explain' (which included guitar work from Jimmy Page and backing vocals by The Ivy League), 'Anyway Anyhow Anywhere' (which became the theme song for TV's *Ready Steady Go*) and 'My Generation'; the last of the three became their anthem. The song's writer, Pete Townshend, said of it, 'It's about old people and young married people', adding 'In a way I'm trying to stop the group getting old – it's the one serious thing we're always talking about.' He was also quoted as saying 'When I'm thirty I'm going to kill myself, 'cos I don't ever want to get old.' Evidently though, he changed his mind. Rolling Stone Brian Jones said at the time 'The Who now occupy the position that The Rolling Stones held after their first few hits. They are the only young group doing something new both visually and musically.' Unlike many of their contemporaries, American success did not come overnight for The Who. In reality, before 'Tommy' made them Stateside superstars, they had only chalked up

"We like to feel we are producing an emotional experience in sound"

Keith Relf of the Yardbirds

75

one previous Top 20 entry, 'I Can See For Miles', in 1969. The Yardbirds, on the other hand, amassed five transatlantic Top 20 hits between 1965 and 1966 – not bad for a group initially written off as 'Stones clones. Indeed it may have been this continual comparison that made them so intent on establishing their own identity and so hell-bent on originality. They almost had contempt for so-called R&B acts who, as lead singer Keith Relf said, 'do songs like "I'm A Hog For You Baby" just like everybody else.' Their first couple of releases were basic R&B, but they only gained recognition from a wider audience when they recorded the much more commercial 'For Your Love'. Their celebrated guitarist Eric Clapton decided this single was the last straw and defected to John Mayall's band (incidentally Mayall had earlier called The Yardbirds 'appalling'). Relf explained their change of of direction by saying 'We don't always record what we like, but first ask ourselves what is going to sell.' He added, almost apologetically, 'We do play a completely different selection of material on club dates, including a lot of Bo Diddley and Buddy Guy numbers - it's really wild stuff.' The group were not over enamoured by their record company's choice of single material, until the release of their self composed 'Still I'm Sad'. Guitarist Chris Dreja said of the record that introduced the rock world to the Gregorian chant, 'I can't tell you how proud we are of this record. It's got originality and that's what we always aim for.' Relf added, 'We like to feel we are producing an emotional experience in sound' - a statement which nowadays would go completely unnoticed, but one that, at the time, sounded somewhat pretentious. This was not the sort of thing other rock stars said about their records. Another British act enrolling in the transatlantic Top 10 club was clean-cut harmony vocal group The Fortunes. They saw themselves as 'providing a contrast to the current craze for beat music. 'We've got nothing against beat music,' vocalist Glen Dale explained, 'but we prefer ballads and slower more tuneful songs.' The public turned a deaf ear to their first four singles, and the disgruntled group seriously contemplated calling it quits. Dame Fortune finally smiled on them when they recorded 'You've Got Your Troubles'. The catchy record climbed into the American Top 10 and was only kept off the top of

"We prefer ballads and slower more tuneful songs"

The Fortunes

The sweet-sounding Fortunes put their money on providing an alternative to the Beat sound of the Boom years

the UK chart by The Beatles' 'Help!'. The success of the single came as a big surprise to the group who did not see its potential, 'We thought, and still think, it was a bit ordinary' they admitted. Their follow-up was the equally infectious 'Here It Comes Again', which Les Reed produced and orchestrated. It too reached the British Top 5, and in America entered the Top 40. They completed their hat-trick of British hits in 1966 with 'This Golden Ring'. Unlike the majority of mid-1960s British groups, The Fortunes returned to the charts long after the initial Beat Boom was over, scoring with 'Here Comes That Rainy Day Feeling', 'Freedom Come Freedom Go' and 'Storm In A Teacup' in the early 1970s.

TRANSATLANTIC BACKLASH

By the end of the summer of 1965 American artists were fighting back. Leading their attack was the most talked about solo performer of the year, singer/songwriter Bob Dylan. As many artists recorded Dylan's material as had covered songs by The Beatles. His folk/rock style and protest oriented lyrics became the trend, and indeed the bandwagon that many lesser talents on both sides of the Atlantic now tried to board. Peter Noone (Herman) was only half joking when he said 'I suppose we will have to do a Dylan song - it seems the only way to get into the charts these days.'

After what had seemed an eternity, American acts were receiving the respect that since early 1964 had seemed the sole prerogative of the British. The garishly garbed LA duo Sonny & Cher were the world's most talked about new artists. They had four singles simultaneously in both the British and US charts. American groups The Byrds, The Walker Brothers, The Shangri-Las and The Righteous Brothers were becoming chart regulars. Other US combos such as The McCoys, Sam The Sham & The Pharaohs, and the Sir Douglas Quintet were also scoring on both sides of the Atlantic. America no longer needed to rely on its R&B contingent, or relative veterans like Elvis, Roy Orbison, Gene Pitney and Jim Reeves to supply its quota of hits in Britain.

'Being British is no guarantee of a full house in America' *Melody Maker* told its readers, explaining that 'The British impact in America is gradually sorting itself out. Some acts still seem able to carve a niche for themselves while others can forget it.' The magazine went on to report 'Even The Beatles and The Dave Clark Five did not pull well in all cities on their recent tours, and The Searchers and The Zombies tours had been 'disappointing'! It added that Herman's Hermits and Tom Jones were 'doing good business', and that after a poor start The Rolling Stones were now attracting bigger crowds.

Meanwhile Britain was also feeling the Beat Boom backlash. The top TV show *Thank Your Lucky Stars*, which for so long had helped set British musical trends, drastically changed its format. A spokesperson for the show said apologetically 'We feel the best of the beat boom is past. Beat group records are not selling in anything like the quantities they were a few months ago. We will be cutting the number of acts on the shows and shall in future use artists with wider appeal. Out goes the parade of long-haired groups and in come family entertainers.' The first of the new style shows starred Liverpool comedian-cum-balladeer Ken Dodd, and middle-of-the-road-singer Petula Clark. The Fortunes were the only actual Beat group featured in the programme.

Dodd and a Diddyman, one of several 'mums and dads' acts that reasserted themselves in the mid-Sixties

> *"We will be cutting the number of acts on the show and shall in future use artists with wider appeal. Out goes the parade of long - haired groups and in come family entertainers"*
>
> *Thank Your Lucky Stars spokesperson*

One of the most distinctive new acts of the year was London-based quartet The Small Faces. The young mod group were fronted by Steve Marriott, who as a soloist had made his first single for Decca in 1963, aged 16. The band charted in 1965 with their debut disc, 'Whatcha Gonna Do About It', which Ian Samwell had written and produced (he also penned Cliff Richard's debut release 'Move It'). They were ideal teenybop fodder and their small faces soon adorned numerous teen magazines. Before Marriott headed for pastures new in 1969, the group had put an impressive ten singles and four albums into the UK Top 20. Their faces, however, did not really fit in the USA, where their only claim to fame came with their tongue-in-cheek psychedelic single, 'Itchycoo Park', which cracked the Top 20 in 1967.

GOOD NEWS

One of the first British composers to write in the Dylan manner was Jonathan King, whose songs cleverly combined messages with catchy choruses. A couple of months after his chart debut as a singer, he had his first hit as a producer with 'It's Good News Week', by Hedgehoppers Anonymous. The quintet, which started life as The Trendsetters, was formed in 1963 by members of the Royal Air Force stationed at Wittering, Sussex. King spotted the group, then known as The Hedgehoppers (an RAF slang term), performing in Cambridge. He liked their vocal arrangements, gave them a selection of his songs to consider and added the word Anonymous to their name. For their debut disc, the group selected 'It's Good News Week' a sarcastic semi-protest song about the bomb dropping, which came complete with a cheerful join-in-and-sing chorus. The record, which utilised several session players, showcased lead vocalist Mick Tinsley and falsetto singer Ray Honeyball. This single jetted straight into the British Top 5 and only narrowly missed the American Top 40. The high-flying group, who championed rhythm and blues, surf music, and Fifties idol Buddy Holly, released another four singles, none of which took off.

**Carnaby Street Mods to a man,
The Small Faces (above)
and student-style folkies
The Silkie (right)**

The folk-flavoured quartet The Silkie were another one-hit wonder in late 1965. The group, who named themselves after a mythical sea creature, first performed together at Hull University. Although they were part of Brian Epstein's world-conquering collection of artists, their Jack Baverstock-produced debut 45, 'Blood Red River', went nowhere. Nevertheless, The Silkie were fortunate in getting The Beatles involved

Headliners at the Fifth National Jazz & Blues Festival at Richmond included The Who, Manfred Mann, Spencer Davis & The Yardbirds

with their next release on the Fontana label, a version of The Beatles' album track from *Help* 'You've Got To Hide Your Love Away'. Not only did John Lennon & Paul McCartney produce the basic track, but also McCartney played rhythm guitar on it and George Harrison joined in on tambourine. The record, which featured lead vocalist Silvia Tatler, stalled at the bottom end of the UK Top 30 but climbed all the way into the American Top 10. The Silkie were one of several British acts whose careers may have suffered when US authorities refused them the correct work permits. The group's subsequent singles and album, The Silkie Sing the Songs Of Bob Dylan, failed to rekindle interest and they very soon vanished into obscurity by way of the folk club circuit.

"We are not changing our approach - I've always maintained that we play Negro pop music and it falls into this catergory."

Spencer Davis on 'Keep On Running'

The Spencer Davis Group (above) with (clockwise from top left) Davis, Muff Winwood, Pete York and Stevie Winwood

GROUP'S GROUP

The final British act to debut in the Top 20 in 1965 were R&B combo The Spencer Davis Group from the Midlands. They were a 'group's group' - praise was heaped on them by their fellow artists long before fame finally found them. Rock celebrities flocked to see them and Ringo Starr, for example, told them he thought their second single, 'I Can't Help It', sounded American - which they took as a great compliment. 'Keep On Running' which, at the outset, was the B-side of

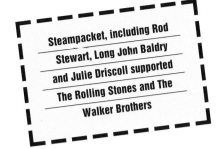

Steampacket, including Rod Stewart, Long John Baldry and Julie Driscoll supported The Rolling Stones and The Walker Brothers

American Blues man Sonny Boy Williamson died. He had been a great influence on the UK R&B scene

1965 TOP SINGLES IN THE UK

	TITLE	ARTIST
1	TEARS	KEN DODD
2	DAY TRIPPER/WE CAN WORK IT OUT	THE BEATLES
3	THE CARNIVAL IS OVER	THE SEEKERS
4	I'M ALIVE	THE HOLLIES
5	HELP!	THE BEATLES
6	TICKET TO RIDE	THE BEATLES
7	LONG LIVE LOVE	SANDIE SHAW
8	THE LAST TIME	THE ROLLING STONES
9	I'LL NEVER FIND ANOTHER YOU	THE SEEKERS
10	GET OFF OF MY CLOUD	THE ROLLING STONES
11	(I CAN'T GET NO) SATISFACTION	THE ROLLING STONES
12	MR. TAMBOURINE MAN	THE BYRDS
13	I GOT YOU BABE	SONNY & CHER
14	CRYING IN THE CHAPEL	ELVIS PRESLEY
15	MAKE IT EASY ON YOURSELF	THE WALKER BROTHERS
16	YEH YEH	GEORGIE FAME
17	THE MINUTE YOU'RE GONE	CLIFF RICHARD
18	YOU'VE LOST THAT LOVIN' FEELIN'	THE RIGHTEOUS BROTHERS
19	IT'S NOT UNUSUAL	TOM JONES
20	GO NOW!	THE MOODY BLUES

their fifth single, turned out to be the hit record they had been waiting for. Davis admitted 'It's a little more commercial than our previous releases', but stressed 'We are not changing our approach – I've always maintained that we play Negro pop music and it falls into this category.' It kept running until it arrived at the top of the UK chart and was the first of five successive Top 20 singles for the classy combo. There is no denying much of the group's success was due to their vocalist/keyboard player Steve Winwood, who was probably the youngest lead singer in the Beat Boom era. He had one of the finest voices in British R&B, which Davis described as 'sounding like a white Negro', anecdotally adding, 'When Steve joined, his voice hadn't even broken and he was able to sing ridiculously high notes.' Proof, if any was needed, that Winwood had almost mastered a black vocal sound came when certain bigoted American pop stations refused to play the group's records until they were assured the band was white! This helped in preventing 'Keep On Running' from reaching the US Top 40. Eventually, though, America too fell under The Spencer Davis Group's spell, and Winwood's classic compositions 'Gimme Some Loving' and 'I'm A Man', both found a home in the US Top 10. The American chart survey at the end of 1965 showed that 14 of the Top 40 singles came from the UK, as did 13 of the year's top 40 acts; an all-time high for the Beat Boom era. However, the only British acts on the last US Top 20 of 1965 were the two who had started the invasion two years earlier; The Beatles and The Dave Clark Five. Clark was enjoying the biggest hit of his career with his chart topping revival of Bobby Day's 1958 undeniably catchy R&B opus 'Over & Over'. It was one of a dozen British records to top the US chart in 1965, a list which astoundingly included four singles that had not even merited a release in the artist's homeland! In the UK itself, singles sales were down a drastic 15% compared to 1964. American acts were staging a commendable comeback in Britain, with half a dozen reaching the pole position during the year (four of whom were making their chart debuts). American songs too were more than holding their own, with half of the year's Top 20 records having been composed on the other side of the Atlantic. The year had seen R&B rapidly losing ground and folk/rock forging ahead. Epstein's empire started to decline while family entertainer (and fellow Liverpudlian) Ken Dodd earned Britain's only 1965 million seller with the decidedly dated MOR ballad, 'Tears'. Dodd, incidentally, was the only act with two singles in the British Top 10 as the year ended.

Britain's two year stranglehold on the transatlantic charts was loosening. America was back in the rock ring and putting up a good fight. As far as the US market was concerned, Britain's Beat Boom had peaked in the spring of 1965 and was now levelling off. By the end of that year British acts were only half as successful in the US Top 100 as they had been eight months earlier.

The times they were a-changin'.

MOODY BLUES

Although the idea of the 'supergroup' was hardly conceived, The Moody Blues could justifiably claim to have been a 'Birmingham supergroup', as four of its five original members had previously worked in successful bands from that area: singer/guitarist Denny Laine had fronted The Diplomats, which also included Bev

David Bowie & The Lower Third
played at the Marquee

'Put Yourself In My Place' by Pye
label act Episode Six was
released, the combo included
Deep Purple's Ian Gillan and
Roger Glover

**The Moody Blues, with future
Wings star Denny Laine (top left)**

Van Morrison hangs on in there as Them take a dip at the Ruislip Lido sometime in August 1963

Bevan (later of The Move and ELO), while drummer Graeme Edge came from Gerry Levene & The Avengers (in which he was a colleague of Roy Wood, later of The Move, Wizzard, ELO, etc), and both keyboard player Mike Pinder and singer/flautist/harmonica man Ray Thomas had been members of El Riot & The Rebels before trying their luck – without success – in Hamburg as members of The Krew Kats. The Moody Blues, formed in May, 1964, were completed by bass player Clint Warwick, and despite the failure of their debut single, the international success of 'Go Now' made them instant stars. However, follow-up singles were much less popular, and by the end of 1966, Warwick had abandoned music and Laine had formed his over-ambitious Electric String Band, which released one excellent single, his composition 'Say You Don't Mind' (which was a UK Top 20 hit for ex- Zombie Colin Blunstone in 1972) before falling apart. The remaining trio recruited bass player/vocalist John Lodge (another ex-member of El Riot & The Rebels) and singer/guitarist/songwriter Justin Hayward, who had served his apprenticeship with Marty Wilde's Wilde Three. The new line-up was at a very low ebb, and after two failed singles, were on the verge of being dropped by Decca, when the company's hi-fi division (which manufactured record players) needed a 'progressive rock' record to demonstrate the capabilities of its hardware. The group were given a few hours in the studio, and intrepidly decided to use the time to showcase their new sound which was dominated by Pinder's mellotron. One of the tracks they recorded was Hayward's ethereal 'Nights In White Satin', which restored them to the UK Top 20 at the end of 1967 after a three year absence. With an accompanying album, 'Days Of Future Passed', the new sound restarted their career, which has been hugely successful (especially in the US) ever since. In 1993, only Pinder of the 'White Satin' line-up of the group was no longer in the band.

THEM

This short-lived but influential Irish R&B band, whose rebellious attitude and music put them on a par with The Rolling Stones and The Animals, were named after a 1954 sci-fi film. Top DJ Jimmy Savile spotted the group and encouraged Decca into signing Them. The quintet had an ever-changing personnel: their best-known line-up was Van (born George Ivan) Morrison (vocals, harmonica), Billy Harrison (lead guitar), Jackie McAuley (piano), Alan Henderson (bass) and Patrick McAuley (drums). Morrison was an urgent and uncompromising vocalist, who had previously tasted success in Germany as a member of The Monarchs. Although many considered him to have almost single handily started the R&B/blues revolution in Ireland, Morrison stressed that Them's repertoire was not limited to those styles of music. 'We don't call ourselves R&B or anything. If we like something we do it' he stressed. Their Dick Rowe-produced debut disc, 'Don't Start Crying Now' (originally cut by blues singer Slim Harpo), failed to win many fans. After backing R&B legend Jimmy Reed on a UK tour, noted US producer (and label owner) Bert Berns took them into the studio. In less than five hours (thanks partly to session men such as Jimmy Page) they recorded 'Baby Please Don't Go' (an old blues standard Morrison had learned from John Lee Hooker's version) and the follow-up 'Here Comes The Night'. Incidentally, the latter song was a Bert Berns composition that label-mate Lulu released first, although she recorded it two weeks later. Both tracks hit the UK Top 10 in 1965, with 'Here Comes The Night' reaching the American Top 40. Personnel problems beset the group and Morrison left, for the second and final time, after a US tour in mid-1966. Soon afterwards Berns reappeared, signed Morrison as a soloist, cut the catchy R&B/rock crossover 'Brown Eyed Girl' and the rest is rock history. The group are probably best remembered for Morrison's composition 'Gloria', which was the B-side of their first hit. It was a hypnotic riffy rocker which became a must-play for every US garage band, and is rightfully regarded in retrospect as a classic of its kind. 'Gloria' became a major American hit in 1966 for The Shadows Of Knight. Surprisingly the song only made its UK chart debut in 1993, when revived by Morrison and his long-time idol, John Lee Hooker.

WHO

The Who were without doubt one of most innovative and influential acts of the 1960s. The ground-breaking London based quartet comprised; Roger Daltrey (vocals), Pete Townshend (guitar), John Entwistle (bass) and Keith Moon (drums). They evolved from a group called The Detours, and were briefly known as The Who before management problems forced them to become The High Numbers. 'We changed our name and altered our style' Daltrey said,'We used to have long hair and maracas and played Jimmy Reed stuff. Real R&B. But when everybody else started playing it, we changed.' In mid-1964, with a new mod image, The High Numbers released 'I'm The Face' (based on R&B star Slim Harpo's 'Got Love If You Want it'). It was arguably the first mod song, and as such it was well received by the music media, although the record buying public chose to ignore it. In late 1964, as The Who, they took up a residency at The Marquee and were billed as 'The Who-Maximum R&B'. They signed to Brunswick in early 1965 and their next release, 'I Can't Explain', hit the Top 10. As it climbed the chart, Daltrey commented 'We do James Brown stuff now, but if everybody else started doing it we'd change again.' Their songwriter-in-chief, Townshend, explained 'We're going to do a new kind of number - if I can churn them out. A New Orleans type of thing, we're getting off the Tamla Motown kick.' The group did alter their sound, adding a rougher, more vicious approach. Their next release, the feedback-filled pop-art pearl 'Anyway Anyhow Anywhere', was also a big British hit, as was 'My Generation' - an unquestionable milestone in rock music. Before the end of the decade, another milestone was reached, when The Who introduced their generation to 'Tommy' and to rock 'opera'. This work was almost universally acclaimed and applauded, even by many of the people that the tearaway teenage Townshend had set out to outrage and ostracise earlier. Although The Who always

1965
TOP SINGLES ARTISTS IN THE UK

1	**THE BEATLES**	PARLOPHONE *UK*
2	**THE ROLLING STONES**	DECCA *UK*
3	**SANDIE SHAW**	PYE *UK*
4	**THE SEEKERS**	COLUMBIA *AUSTRALIAN*
5	**THE ANIMALS**	COLUMBIA *UK*
6	**CLIFF RICHARD**	COLUMBIA *UK*
7	**THE YARDBIRDS**	COLUMBIA *UK*
8	**THE HOLLIES**	PARLOPHONE *UK*
9	**KEN DODD**	COLUMBIA *UK*
10	**BOB DYLAN**	CBS *US*
11	**THE KINKS**	PYE *UK*
12	**MANFRED MANN**	HMV *UK*
13	**GENE PITNEY**	STATESIDE *US*
14	**TOM JONES**	DECCA *UK*
15	**THE BYRDS**	CBS *US*
16	**MARIANNE FAITHFUL**	DECCA *UK*
17	**P.J.PROBY**	LIBERTY *US*
18	**HERMAN'S HERMITS**	COLUMBIA *UK*
19	**THE WHO**	BRUNSWICK *UK*
20	**SONNY & CHER**	ATLANTIC *US*

The early 'Yardies' with Clapton, Samwell-Smith, Relf, McCartey and Dreja, and (below) the ever-smiling Fortunes

seemed on the verge of a break-up, they outlasted nearly all of their contemporaries and became one of the all time top selling record acts in the world. The platinum-plated group (minus Moon, who died in 1978) officially split in 1983, reunited briefly for *Live Aid* in 1985 and again in 1989 for a US tour, which earned them a staggering $30 million.

YARDBIRDS

The Yardbirds, who were among the most influential figures in the Beat Boom era, evolved in 1963 from The Metropolitan Blues Band. Their earliest line-up was Keith Relf (vocals, harmonica), Paul Samwell-Smith (bass), Chris Dreja (guitar), Tony 'Top' Topham (guitar) and Jim McCarty (drums), with Eric Clapton (real name Eric Clapp) replacing Topham before the end of the year. At first, The Yardbirds' instrumentation and sound may have been reminiscent of The Rolling Stones, but in their relatively short existence, this London based band more than earned their place in any Rock Music Hall of Fame. They had the unenviable task of taking over the Stones' residency at the Crawdaddy Club in Richmond, yet, the 'most blueswailing Yardbirds' as they were tagged, won over the predominantely mod audence with a carefully chosen collection of obscure US R&B songs. They first recorded in late 1963 as the backing group for the aged American blues legend, Sonny Boy Williamson. The fashionable fivesome's first solo releases on Columbia were the blues standards, 'I Wish You Would' (originally by Billy Boy Arnold) and 'Good Morning Little School Girl' (previously recorded by Don & Bob), which sold reasonably well, but it was their third single, the blatantly commercial 'For Your Love', which started their string of successes on both sides of the Atlantic. Graham Gouldman had composed the song for his group, The Mockingbirds, but after seeing The Yardbirds on The Beatles 1964 Christmas Show, decided it would make more sense for them to record it. The single topped the chart (at about the time that Clapton quit and was replaced by Jeff Beck) and their two Gouldman-composed follow-ups, 'Heart Full Of Soul' and 'Evil Hearted You', also made the Top 10. Once they had a couple of hits tucked under their belts, the band were allowed more input into their recordings, and indeed were encouraged to experiment and be more adventurous in the studios. From this new found freedom came such revolutionary rock tracks as 'Still I'm Sad', 'Shapes Of Things' and 'Over Under Sideways Down'. The Yardbirds, who by mid-1966

Marty Wilde and Justin Hayward recorded with Wilde's wife as the Wilde Three

'Baby's Back In Town' was the only release by Ten Foot Five, an act that contained half the Troggs

included Jimmy Page (of whom Relf said 'probably has more ideas about different effects produced from a guitar than any other musician in the country), pioneered many of the technical guitar innovations of the time, including the use of feedback and fuzz tone. They helped shape the direction of late 1960s popular music and laid a firm foundation for heavy metal. The group started to lose their way in 1967 and split the following year. Jimmy Page then formed the New Yardbirds, who were soon re-named Led Zeppelin.

FORTUNES

The Fortunes were a top-notch harmony vocal outfit. They initially performed as The Cliftones, and featured vocalists Rod Allen (real name Rodney Bainbridge), Glen Dale (real name Richard Garforth) and Barry Pritchard. In 1963, the group made their recording debut on Decca with a revival of The Jamies' compelling two-time US hit 'Summertime Summertime'. Despite heavy radio play, their follow-up 'Caroline' (the theme song to Pirate ship Radio Caroline) narrowly missed the chart, while their next two singles sank without trace. The act's commercial breakthrough finally came with Roger Greenaway and Roger Cook's memorable sing-a-long song, 'You've Got Your Troubles', which became a major transatlantic hit in 1965. Later that year, The Fortunes arrived in the USA for TV and live work, only to find the Immigration Department had refused their television work permit. Apart from losing an estimated £10,000 when their nine prime TV spots were cancelled, the progress of their follow-up, 'Here It Comes Again', was almost certainly hampered in the States. The well-groomed, smartly dressed group scored their third UK Top 20 hit in early 1966 with another appealing Greenaway and Cook composition, 'This Golden Ring'. Shortly afterwards Dale decided to try a solo career, but neither he nor the group returned to the charts that decade. In 1971, after five years of fairly routine cabaret, club work, and jingle recording, The Fortunes signed to Capitol and were fortunate enough to have a second taste of fame. They returned to the American Top 20 with Greenaway & Cook's 'Here Comes That Rainy Day Feeling', and shortly afterwards reappeared in the British Top10 with the equally engaging pop ditties 'Freedom Come Freedom Go' (another Greenaway & Cook song) and 'Storm In A Teacup' written for them by singer/songwriter Lynsey De Paul.

SMALL FACES

If The Who were widely regarded as the premier 'mod' group, The Small Faces were their only real rivals for that accolade. The band was formed in the summer of 1965 by bassist Ronnie 'Plonk' Lane and drummer Kenny Jones (from The Outcasts), who recruited organist Jimmy Winston, and the initial line-up was completed by singer and guitarist Steve Marriott. He had fronted Steve Marriott & The Moments (which also included John Weider, who was later in The Animals and later still in Family) and was an ex-child actor, who had appeared as The Artful Dodger in the Lionel Bart musical *Oliver*. The quartet took its name from the fact that Lane, Marriott & Jones were short in stature, and highly respected Mods were often referred to as 'faces'. After their initial chart hit, 'Whatcha Gonna Do About It', Winston left to form his own unsuccessful

Peter Noone (Herman) met with Elvis, during a US tour on which the opening act for Herman's Hermits was the Zombies

September 1965, The Small Faces face the television cameras

	TITLE	ARTIST
1	(I CAN'T GET NO) SATISFACTION	THE ROLLING STONES
2	YESTERDAY	THE BEATLES
3	TURN! TURN! TURN!	THE BYRDS
4	MRS BROWN YOU'VE GOT A LOVELY DAUGHTER	HERMAN'S HERMITS
5	YOU'VE LOST THAT LOVIN' FEELIN'	THE RIGHTEOUS BROTHERS
6	I CAN'T HELP MYSELF	THE FOUR TOPS
7	DOWNTOWN	PETULA CLARK
8	HELP!	THE BEATLES
9	I GOT YOU BABE	SONNY & CHER
10	THIS DIAMOND RING	GARY LEWIS & THE PLAYBOYS
11	STOP! IN THE NAME OF LOVE	THE SUPREMES
12	GET OFF OF MY CLOUD	THE ROLLING STONES
13	HELP ME, RHONDA	THE BEACH BOYS
14	I HEAR A SYMPHONY	THE SUPREMES
15	MY GIRL	THE TEMPTATIONS
16	I'M TELLING YOU NOW	FREDDIE & THE DREAMERS
17	EIGHT DAYS A WEEK	THE BEATLES
18	HANG ON SLOOPY	THE McCOYS
19	MR. TAMBOURINE MAN	THE BYRDS
20	EVE OF DESTRUCTION	BARRY McGUIRE

The Spencer Davis Group (opposite) in an atmospheric shot by top rock photographer Gered Mankovitz

group, Winston's Fumbs, and was replaced by Ian McLagan (ex-Boz & The Boz People), who was also as small as his new colleagues. The group's first UK Top 3 hit was 'Sha La La La Lee', a slice of classic bubblegum written by Kenny Lynch & Mort Shuman, which was followed by the first hit written by the Marriott/Lane team, 'Hey Girl'. A third 1966 hit 'All Or Nothing', topped the UK chart, and a fourth, 'My Mind's Eye', made the Top 5, but the group were unhappy with Decca, the label to which they were signed, and moved to Rolling Stones manager Andrew Loog Oldham's recently launched Immediate label. Their first four singles for the new label, 'Here Comes The Nice', 'Itchycoo Park' (the first hit to use a phased drum sound), 'Tin Soldier' (on which fellow Immediate artist P. P. Arnold added her soulful backing vocals) and 'Lazy Sunday' (a classic cockney record) were all sizeable hits, and the group also released a most adventurous album, 'Ogden's Nut Gone Flake'. This boasted a round sleeve which looked like a one-dimerisional tobacco tin, and it topped the British album chart. Unfortunately, it was to be their final moment of glory, as in early 1969, Marriott and Peter Frampton (ex-The Herd) launched Humble Pie. The remaining trio initially recruited Ron Wood (ex-Artwoods, Creation, etc.) and later Rod Stewart, at which point they changed their name to The Faces, and enjoyed further success during the early 1970s.

SPENCER DAVIS GROUP

This Birmingham band were formed in 1963, when one-time skiffler Spencer Davis (guitar) teamed with Pete York (drums) and two ex-trad band members, 15 year-old Steve Winwood (vocals, keyboard) and his brother Mervyn 'Muff' (bass). The R&B quartet initially called themselves by the somewhat unoriginal handle of The Rhythm & Blues Quartet before adopting their leader's name. They soon became one of the most talked about and admired bands in Britian, but record success did not come overnight. The group got the thumbs down from Decca, and their debut Fontana outing, 'Dimples' (a John Lee Hooker blues song), did little. Their next three releases: 'I Can't Stand It' (originally by the Soul Sisters), 'Every Little Bit Hurts' (a soul ballad first cut by Brenda Holloway) and 'Strong Love' (released previously by US group The Malibus), narrowly missed the Top 30. The quartet's long overdue breakthrough came when they recorded a song written by bluebeat artist Jackie Edwards, 'Keep On Running'. Both this single and their

equally irresistible Edwards-penned follow-up, 'Somebody Help Me', topped the UK chart. 1966 was a dream year for The Spencer Davis Group; in Britain they had four Top 20 singles, three Top 10 albums and were voted Best New Group in the NME Poll. It was also the year that the exuberant 'Gimme Some Loving' (which owed a little to Memphis singer/songwriter Homer Banks' 'A Lot Of Love') became their first transatlantic Top 10 entry. Davis, like Manfred Mann before him, was not the focal point of the group which bore his name; talented singer Steve Winwood took that role. This meant the image of The Spencer Davis Group was different from most other Beat Boom bands; as keyboard-bound Winwood put it, 'we don't have a guy standing at the front and waggling his rear.' When Winwood left in 1967 to launch Traffic, the band's days were numbered. Muff Winwood went on to become an extremely successful A&R man in Britain (working with CBS/Sony), while little brother Steve became one of the world's best respected solo recording artists.

1965
TOP SINGLES ARTISTS IN THE US

1	**HERMAN'S HERMITS**	MGM *UK*
2	**THE BEATLES**	CAPITOL *UK*
3	**THE SUPREMES**	MOTOWN *US*
4	**GARY LEWIS & THE PLAYBOYS**	LIBERTY *US*
5	**THE ROLLING STONES**	LONDON *UK*
6	**THE DAVE CLARK FIVE**	EPIC *UK*
7	**THE RIGHTEOUS BROTHERS**	PHILLES *US*
8	**THE BEACH BOYS**	CAPITOL *US*
9	**THE BYRDS**	COLUMBIA *US*
10	**SONNY & CHER**	ATCO *US*
11	**THE FOUR TOPS**	MOTOWN *US*
12	**PETULA CLARK**	WARNER *UK*
13	**ELVIS PRESLEY**	RCA *US*
14	**ROGER MILLER**	SMASH *US*
15	**THE TEMPTATIONS**	GORDY *US*
16	**MARVIN GAYE**	TAMLA *US*
17	**JAY & THE AMERICANS**	UA *US*
18	**THE McCOYS**	BANG *US*
19	**THE FOUR SEASONS**	PHILIPS *US*
20	**BOB DYLAN**	COLUMBIA *US*

Thank you girl

FEMALE SOLOISTS

In the 1950s, it seemed standard practice for British female singers to go on stage dressed as if for a ball at Buckingham Palace. There were few rockin' ladies and none of those made their mark on the charts. In general, the girls and ladies were more restrained musically than their male counterparts - rock revolutionised many things, but the majority of female artists were almost unaffected by its arrival.

The first successful new British female singer of the 1960s was 14 year old schoolgirl Helen Shapiro, the possessor of a distinctive, if slightly masculine, voice, who dressed a mite more street-wise than her well-preened predecessors. Shapiro, who was initially promoted in the press as 'Britain's Brenda Lee', was an instant success in the UK, and her first four singles all went into the Top 5. Her material was original and catchy, and had she come along later she could have had a hat full of American hits. However, she only managed one week at the bottom of the US Top 100 in 1961 with her bouncy British chart topper, 'Walkin' Back To Happiness'. Many teenage British girls followed in Shapiro's footsteps, and a nice-girl-next-door image ruled in the UK in the first years of the Swingin' Sixties. The only British female to make an impression on the US chart at the time was another 14 year-old, actress Hayley Mills, whose cute 1961 transatlantic Top 20 hit, 'Let's Get Together', came from her film, *The Parent Trap*. Although Mills sported a mop top haircut in the film, and her hit had a distinct 'yeah yeah yeah' refrain, it is not thought to have influenced The Beatles!

Only five girls managed to make their UK chart debuts in 1963, the first year of the Beat Boom in Britain: Julie Grant, Maureen Evans, Billie Davis, Kathy Kirby and Dora Bryan.

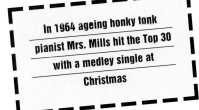

In 1964 ageing honky tonk pianist Mrs. Mills hit the Top 30 with a medley single at Christmas

THE RIGHT MATERIAL

Julie Grant was a 16 year from Leeds, who in 1960, when aged 14, beat Helen Shapiro in a talent competition at Butlin's Holiday Camp in Brighton. She had a minor hit with her fourth single, an up-tempo cover of Carole King's song, 'Up On The Roof', which also charted for The Drifters and Kenny Lynch. Grant, who appeared on The Rolling Stones' first UK tour, returned to the Top 30 with two more Pye singles, 'Count On Me' (1963) penned by producer Tony Hatch and 'Come To Me' (1964), before being replaced by the new-breed of female vocalist, who in many cases were older than her.

Maureen Evans from Cardiff, Wales, started in 1958 by recording cover versions for Woolworth's budget priced label, Embassy. A year later she moved to the full price label, Oriole, but continued to rely heavily on American songs for her repertoire. In 1960 her cover of Toni Fisher's unusual US success, 'The Big Hurt', was nearly the big hit for her. She temporarily took time out to have a baby, and on returning in 1963 teamed up with John Schroeder, discoverer of Helen Shapiro and writer of most of her hits,. She hit her commercial peak when he produced the humable 'Like I Do', which took her into the UK Top 5 . The song was based on Ponchielli's classical composition, 'Dance Of The Hours' (as was' Allan Sherman's comic 1963 hit 'Hello Muddah Hello Faddah'), and it had been a European success earlier for Nancy Sinatra. Evans nearly returned to the big time in 1964 with her interpretation of 'I Love How You Love Me', a million seller for The Paris Sisters. When asked about her recordings she made an interesting point, 'Writers always seem to turn out plenty of songs for the boys, but girl singers are treated unfairly - it's difficult to find the right material.' She concluded by saying things were changing and that 1963 was going to be a good year as 'Everyone is starting to realise that girls are just as capable of singing hit songs as boys.'

WISHIN' AND HOPIN'

Strong-voiced Surrey-born singer Billie Davis (real name Carol Hedges) first charted as the female foil for singer/actor Mike Sarne on his 1962 hit, 'Will I What'. She was groomed for stardom by manager and producer Robert Stigwood (later mananger of acts like The Bee Gees), who decided not to release her first solo record, the Joe Meek-produced and Tornados-backed 'Merry Go Round'. Davis had a well deserved five minutes of fame when her first solo single, an exciting interpretation of 'Tell Him', an American smash for The Exciters, reached the UK Top 20. When asked in early 1963 about her recordings, teenager Davis said 'The important thing is to have the American Sound. I just love that sort of sound - and Robert Stigwood knows how to get it.' Stigwood commented 'I have never heard a girl in Britain who has that American Sound. I mean she really has the Brenda Lee-Little Eva approach to her singing.'

> ## "Everyone is starting to realise that girls are just as capable of singing hit songs as boys"
> ### Maureen Evans

US soul singer Doris Troy, who covered The Small Faces' 'Whatcha Gonna Do About It', took up residence in the UK

(opposite) Billie Davis on the release of 'Angel Of The Morning' which was beaten to the chart by the P.P.Arnold version (below) Maureen Evans

Davis, who chose her name because she admired Billie Anthony and Sammy Davis Jr., was arguably the first British female singer to see herself as an R&B performer. She continued to record for many years on numerous labels but never fulfilled her early promise. Kathy Kirby's lively vocal version of the No. 1 instrumental hit from The Shadows, 'Dance On', helped establish her as a hit maker in autumn, 1963. During the next nine months this Marilyn Monroe-lookalike was voted Top British Female Singer in the *NME* poll, and put a further three singles in the UK Top 20. In 1965, her single, 'The Way Of Love', appeared briefly in the American chart.

The final female to debut in the British Top 20 in 1963 was forty year-old Dora Bryan (born Dora Broadbent). She was a well-known actress/comedienne who was regularly seen on British TV. She had also appeared in several films including the forgettable *Mother Riley Meets The Vampire* and the memorable

Female archetypes for the Swinging Sixties: Dusty Springfield (above), Cilla Black (below), Sandie Shaw (top, opposite) and Lulu

A Taste of Honey. Bryan briefly tasted chart fame with the timely novelty, 'All I Want For Christmas Is A Beatle', on Fontana. Perhaps not surprisingly, her follow-up, another hero worshipping waxing, 'Oh, Oh, Oh, Oh Seven' sold about that many copies. It seems very chauvinistic now, but in the early 1960s the record business treated female singers almost like second class citizens. The simple reason was, as *RM* put it, 'Girls buy most of the records, therefore they won't buy discs by girls. While girls may be very nice to look at, the fans do not regard them as being worth the money to listen to.' Like many other opinions of the early 1960s, this one was to change dramatically by mid-decade. 1964 was probably the most fruitful year for British female singers in the entire history of rock music. In that 12 month period Dusty Springfield, Cilla Black, Lulu and Sandie Shaw joined the honour roll of hit makers. It was also the year that Julie Rogers and Millie (Small) had a brief fling with chart fame, Marianne Faithfull first made her mark, and that formidable chanteuse, Petula Clark, finally found fame on the other side of the Atlantic. In early 1963, Cliff Richard & The Shadows tagged Dusty Springfield 'The White Negress', which delighted Dusty, 'You can't get a more pleasing comment when you really go for groups like The Shirelles and The Crystals' she commented. Her first solo single, after poll winning folk/country trio The Springfields split, was the infectious hook-packed pop/R&B opus, 'I Only Want To Be With You'. The song, which was a complete change of direction for her, was the first ever heard on British TV's longest running pop show, *Top Of The Pops*. Springfield also had significant successes with Bacharach & David's compositions, 'I Just Don't Know What To Do With Myself' (originally cut by Tommy Hunt) and 'Wishin' And Hopin'' (first recorded by Dionne Warwick). In 1964 her recording of the former reached the UK Top 3, while the latter became her first US Top 10 entry. Also that year, Springfield scooped the award for Top Female British Artist in the *NME*

"I don't like sequins, frills and fussy fussy dresses, they make me look like a fairy queen on top of a Christmas tree, and that simply isn't me"

Cilla Black

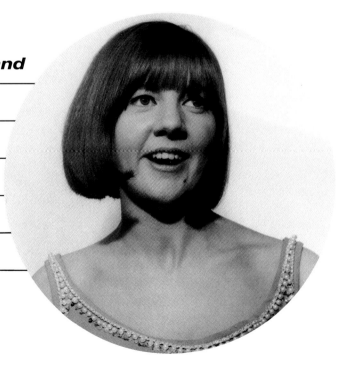

> ### *"While girls may be very nice to look at, the*
> ### *fans do not regard them as being worth the*
> ### *money to listen to"*
>
> ### *Record Mirror*

Poll, and in 1965 not only held that title but also became the first Briton to win the World's Top Female award. The second Liverpool lady (after Beryl Marsden) to be launched into the pop firmament was Cilla Black, a part time singer-cum-cloakroom attendant at the famous Cavern Club. Brian Epstein realised her star potential and signed her for management. He quickly placed her with producer George Martin at Parlophone, put her on tour with The Beatles, and lined up a *Ready Steady Go* appearance on the release day of her debut single, 'Love Of The Loved'. Epstein described Black as 'Britain's most exciting new beat songstress,' and called her 'The gal with the bright red hair and the jet black voice.' Black, who said she preferred to sing 'good numbers recorded by lesser known American artists,' cemented herself as a major artist when her rendition of Dionne Warwick's American breakthrough single, 'Anyone Who Had A Heart', sold almost a million copies in the UK alone. She said of Warwick's waxing 'I love her version, but the song was too good for me to turn down.' Cilla helped to smash the stereotype of how a girl singer should dress. 'I don't like sequins, frills and fussy fussy dresses' she said, 'they make me look like a fairy queen on top of a Christmas tree, and that simply isn't me.' Although she never managed the upper reaches of the American charts, she certainly had a lorra lorra (Liverpudlian for 'a lot of') British hits in the 1960s.

SIXTIES GIRLS

The youngest new British female star that year was 15 year old Scots lass Lulu, whose stage name was dreamed up by her manager Tony Gordon. After being rejected by EMI (a company she later joined) Lulu & The Luvvers signed with Decca, where Peter Sullivan produced her records. Their first release revived the Isley Brothers' classic (though under-rated in the UK) rock'n'roll masterpiece 'Shout'. Lulu, who admitted she had 'copied the Isley Brothers version,' gave a spirited and upbeat performance, aptly described by a reviewer as having 'an earthy authentic R&B feel.' It rightfully put her into the UK Top 10 and helped her win the *RM* award for Most Promising Act of 1964. She added to her mid-1960s Top 10 tally with 'Leave A Little Love' in 1965 and Neil Diamond's perky, 'The Boat That I Row', two years later. Lulu's biggest hit also came in 1967, when the moving ballad, 'To Sir With Love', which was the B-side of her British success 'Let's Pretend' (composed by US singer/songwriter Paul Evans), topped the American chart. Britain's most successful female manager in the 1960s was almost certainly Eve Taylor. It was Taylor who spotted Sandie Shaw's potential and signed her with Tony Hatch at Pye Records in 1964. Like Cilla Black, it was her second single that turned the tall, model-like singer into a star. Also like Cilla, it took a Burt Bacharach and Hal

David song to do the trick. In Shaw's case, her maiden hit came with a commercial cover of Lou Johnson's minor US success, '(There's) Always Something There To Remind Me', which took her to the top spot. Her next three singles and her debut album, Sandie, also reached The Top 5 in 1965, the year that she picked up the award for Top British Female Singer from *MM*. Shaw, who made bare feet fashionable, and, perhaps more than any other girl vocalist personified the 1960s British look, never managed to break through in the States.

BRIDES AND BLUE BEAT

Three British based young women who did achieve US success in 1964 were Julie Rogers, Millie and Marianne Faithfull. Julie Rogers (born Julie Rolls), hailed, like Tommy Steele, from Bermondsey in London, and joined Teddy Foster's Band as a vocalist in the early 1960s. Her first single, a revival of Doris Day's 1948 hit, 'It's Magic', failed to do the trick, but her next release, an update of The Chordettes' minor 1956 US hit, 'The Wedding', marched into the top 10 on both sides of the Atlantic in 1964. Johnny Franz produced Rogers' recording of the timeless betrothal ballad, which became synonymous with nuptials. It continued to sell well long after its chart honeymoon was over and has allegedly sold over seven million copies world-wide. Rogers was not a rocker, but was a classy cabaret performer, and among those who sang her praises were Roy Orbison (he tipped her for US fame) and Benny Hill, who simply described her as 'a cracker.' Her follow-up, 'Like A Child', narrowly missed the UK Top 20, and future releases including a revival of another 1950s marital melody, 'Hawaiian Wedding Song', failed to take her up the chart aisle again.

Effervescent and bouncy Jamaican-born Millie Small, known simply as Millie in the UK, first recorded as half of a duo with Roy Panton, and their debut disc, 'We'll Meet', was a West Indian hit. Chris Blackwell, owner of the then small independant label, Island, spotted her potential, brought the 16 year old to Britain and licensed her records to Fontana, feeling that the Island label was too small to get big hits. For her second UK recorded single she cut 'My Boy Lollipop', a song composed by US doo-wopper Bobby Spencer (who also wrote 'I'm Not A

A female quartet known as The Mysteries released 'Give Me Rhythm & Blues' on Decca in 1964

East Londoner Julie Rogers (left) and West Indian Millie Small both graced the charts memorably though briefly

Juvenile Delinquent' for The Teenagers) and originally released in 1956 by Barbie Gaie. Millie's Blue Beat (the Jamaican forerunner of Reggae) treatment of this extremely catchy compostion took it to the runner-up position on both sides of the Atlantic, and thereby introduced the pop world to this unique West Indian rhythm. The similar sounding 'Sweet William' returned her to the transatlantic Top 40, but future recordings, including Blue Beat versions of other early US rock'n'roll songs such as 'See You Later Alligator' and 'Bloodshot Eyes', had few takers. For the record, her million selling single is said to feature Rod Stewart on harmonica. Be that as it may, the single certainly helped to keep Island Records afloat.

BLONDE, BRIT AND BEAT

Marianne Faithfull was another British act who achieved some American success to match her domestic haul of four Top 20 hits in 1964/5. From the point of view of the media, she was perfection personified - long blonde hair, demure but sexy, and most importantly, Mick Jagger's girlfriend. It was The Rolling Stones vocalist (together with Keith Richards) who penned the virginal-voiced folk-flavoured vocalist's initial hit, the haunting ballad, 'As Tears Go By'. A series of much publicised personal problems hastened the end of her chart career. However, over the years she has accumulated many faithful fans, who have elevated her more recent recordings to virtual cult status.

Petula Clark was the most popular British female singer in the States in the Swinging Sixties. Clark, who had remained in the British public's eye since her first broadcast as a precocious nine year old in 1942, finally broke through in America in early 1965 when 'Downtown' topped the US chart (the first single by a British female to make No. 1 since 1952), and went on to pick up the Grammy for Best Rock'n'Roll Record Of The Year. Before the end of 1968, she had amassed 15 Top 40 singles, most of which Tony Hatch, her prolific producer, penned. The singer, who incidentally had 20 film appearances under her belt before the start of the 1960s, went down a storm Stateside. Reviews of her debut at top New York niterie The Copacabana proclaimed 'She suggests an amalgamated Judy Garland, Julie Andrews and Edith Piaf with a generous amount of her own magic.' Another critic noted 'Her face is fascinating and her voice is louder than all The Beatles put together,' whilst the New York Post simply said 'That's the greatest show I've seen in 20 years at the Copacabana!' America's DJs agreed and voted her the Most Popular Female Singer in the USA in 1966.

Well-remembered one-hit wonder Twinkle (above) had a fleeting fame compared to the lengthy career of Petula Clark

The Beat Boom may have loosened the chains that for many years had restrained British female singers, but there were still some shackles to be broken before UK woman songwriters were accepted in the same way as top tunesmiths like Carole King, Ellie Greenwich and Cynthia Weil in America. The first British female singer/songwriter to score in the rock era was 17 year old Twinkle (real name Lynn Ripley), who signed to Decca in 1964. Twinkle's debut disc, 'Terry', was a death ditty about a biker (as had been Ellie Greenwich's earlier hit song, 'Leader Of the Pack', a million seller for The Shangri-Las). Dick Rowe produced her records and Phil Coulter (who later penned chart toppers like 'Puppet On A String' for Sandie Shaw and 'Congratulations' for Cliff Richard) was her musical arranger. She followed this UK Top 3 entry with another self-composed song 'Golden Lights', which almost doubled her Top 20 tally. Twinkle, who is remembered in the UK with far more respect that most 'little stars', also recorded other 'boy' songs, 'Tommy' and 'Poor Old Johnny', but neither of them took her to the same heights

Husband and wife songwriting/production team Jackie Trent and Tony Hatch

as 'Terry'. In the late 1970s, Twinkle re-recorded her biker's anthem, but this time 'Terry' failed to drive her up the charts. Like Sandie Shaw, Morrissey temporarily brought her back into the limelight in 1987, when his group, The Smiths, revived 'Golden Lights'.

CRITICAL ACCLAIM

The most successful British female songwriter of the 1960s was surely Staffordshire born Jackie Trent, who had started as a professional singer in the late 1950s. Her first records for Oriole in 1962 vanished without trace as did her initial singles on Pye. However, in 1965, 'Where Are You Now (My Love)', a timeless MOR ballad that she had written as a TV theme with her producer (and future husband) Tony Hatch, topped the UK chart, and gave her the only big vocal hit of her career. Multi-talented Trent then concentrated on her song writing, and together with Hatch penned several of Petula Clark's best sellers including 'I Couldn't Live Without Your Love' and 'Don't Sleep In The Subway'. She also co-wrote the semi-standard 'Joanna', as well as several other well-known TV themes, including the one from the top rated Australian soap opera *Neighbours*.

All-in-all the Beat Boom was very kind to British female singers, opening doors for them on both sides of the Atlantic. In the UK, the Top five female singers of the era were all local ladies: Cilla Black, Dusty Springfield, Sandie Shaw, Petula Clark and Marianne Faithfull. While in America, where the Top 10 album chart had remained a no-go area for all UK woman excluding Julie 'Mary Poppins' Andrews, Petula Clark was the most successful female singles artist between 1964-1966, and only Frank's daughter Nancy Sinatra stopped the more critically acclaimed Dusty Springfield taking the runner-up position.

KATHY KIRBY

Convent educated Kathy Kirby learned her trade from the veteran big band leader Ambrose, who added her to his band when she was only 16 and managed her throughout her most prosperous period. After going solo in the late 1950s, she worked in cabaret in Britain and across Europe (including a six month residency at the swanky Blue Angel Club in London's Mayfair), and in the early 1960s successfully toured the UK with both Cliff Richard and Duane Eddy. The MOR-slanted singer had two little remembered releases on Pye before joining Decca in 1962. She is best known for her hits 'Dance On' (penned by UK group The Avons), 'Secret Love', an update of Doris Day's 1954 chart topping ballad, 'You're The One' and 'Let Me Go Lover', a dramatic ballad which in 1955 had given Joan Weber her only taste of fame. Kathy Kirby had her own TV series in 1964 and represented Britain in the 1965 Eurovision Song Contest .

DUSTY SPRINGFIELD

Dusty Springfield, who was born Mary O'Brien in London, was a member of the late 1950s female trio The Lana Sisters, who released a handful of singles on Fontana. In 1960 she formed folk/country/pop trio The Springfields with brother Dion (better known as Tom) and Tim Field. They were not only extremely popular in their homeland (voted Top Group of 1961 & 1962 in the *NME* Poll), but were also the first British vocal group to crack the US Top 20. In 1966, the singer, who had become something of a role model for many

Dusty Springfield (left) on the set of *Ready Steady Go !*,

British teenage girls with her unmistakable blonde beehive hairdo and her heavy black eye make-up, starred in her own BBC TV series, *Dusty* (which ran for two seasons). Springfield was a regular in the British and US charts, and among her stockpile of hit singles were the transatlantic successes 'You Don't Have To Say You Love Me' in 1966 (a beautiful ballad that also hit for Elvis Presley in 1971), and the soulful Memphis-recorded side, 'Son Of A Preacher Man', in 1969. In all she has amassed 17 UK and six US Top 20 singles, and eight Top 40 albums in Britain. She moved to the US in the 1970s, and made the Transatlantic Top 10 in 1988 in collaboration with The Pet Shop Boys.

CILLA BLACK

Liverpool's Cilla Black (born Priscilla White) was one of the most successful female singers in the UK in the 1960s - a decade when 13 of her singles and three of her albums reached the UK Top 20. In the early 1960s, Swingin' Cilla White (as she was known) often performed songs like 'Alley Oop', 'Fever' and 'Boys' at the Cavern Club, backed by groups like Kingsize Taylor & The Dominoes, The Big Three and The Beatles. Manager Brian Epstein liked her singing style and 'girl-next-door' image, and she became his first female client. Black's debut disc, 'Love Of The Loved' (a previously unrecorded Beatles ballad), cracked the Top 30, and

the personality-packed Scouser had her first major hit with the follow-up, 'Anyone Who Had A Heart', in 1964. Her version of this emotion-charged Bacharach & David song topped the chart, as did her follow up 45, 'You're My World' (a romantic Italian song which was her only US Top 40 entry). Black's other major Beat Boom hits included Lennon & McCartney's tuneful 'It's For You', a rousing cover of 'You've Lost That Lovin' Feelin' ' (which narrowly but deservedly lost a UK chart battle with The Righteous Brothers original version), 'Love's Just A Broken Heart' and the memorable film theme, 'Alfie'. This unmistakable vocalist soon became a top notch all-round-entertainer, starring at such prestigious venues as the London Palladium and the Persian Room in New York's plush Plaza hotel. Black, who has never been out of the spotlight in Britain, is now one of the country's best known TV celebrities, hosting the very popular shows, *Surprise Surprise* and *Blind Date* (the British version of *Dating Game*).

LULU

Lulu was born Marie McDonald Lawrie near Glasgow, Scotland. Her debut disc, 'Shout', which also featured her band, The Luvvers (previously known as The Gleneagles), was an instant hit and the first of her nine British Top 20 singles in the 1960s. In 1966, the bouncy and effervescent performer, who said her tastes in music were gospel, soul and R&B, split from The Luvvers. Lulu only had one big American hit in the swinging 60s - but what a lulu of a hit it was. 'To Sir With Love', which was the touching theme to a Sidney Poitier film in which she appeared, reached No. 1 and sold well over a million, going on to become the biggest single in the USA that year. She signed with hit producer Mickie Most in 1967, and moved to Columbia Records. The following year she hosted her own successful TV variety series, and was voted the Top British Female Singer in the *RM* Poll. In the last year of the decade, she married Bee Gee Maurice Gibb and won the European Song Contest for Britain. The winning song, 'Boom Bang-A-Bang', was an archetypal Eurovision song, which in retrospect did little for her career. During the 1970s Lulu recorded for various labels with varying degrees of

In 1964 Dusty Springfield hosted *The Sound Of Motown* an ITV special featuring The Supremes, Martha & The Vandellas, The Miracles, The Temptations and Stevie Wonder

Cilla Black in full showbiz mode at a Royal Variety Performance

success, her biggest hit of the decade coming in 1974 with the David Bowie produced and written single, 'The Man Who Sold The World', which returned her to the UK Top 3. In 1986 the sales of her re-recording of 'Shout' were combined with those of her original version, which pushed the song back into the UK Top 10. There was also a resurgence in her career in 1993, when she returned to the UK Top 20 as a vocalist with 'Independence', as a songwriter when 'I Don't Wanna Fight' was a top transatlantic hit for Tina Turner, and guesting on 'Relight My Fire', the UK hit by Take That.

SANDIE SHAW

Adam Faith reportedly discovered Essex girl Sandie Shaw (real name Sandra Goodrich), when she auditioned unexpectedly for him after one of his shows. Eve Taylor, her astute manager who also managed Faith, re-named her and also came up with the idea that she should always perform in her bare feet. Shaw's first single, the Chris Andrews composed 'As Long As You're Happy', failed to penetrate the chart, but her second release, the scintillating '(There's) Always Something There To Remind Me', in late 1964 more than made up for that by going all the way to No 1. Shaw then wisely returned to Chris Andrews' material, and he duly supplied her with such Top 10 hits as 'Girl Don't Come', 'I'll Stop At Nothing', the chart topping 'Long Live Love', 'Message Understood' and 'Tomorrow'. Shaw, who barely put a foot wrong in the mid-1960s, completed her hat-trick of No. 1 hits in 1967 with the Eurovision Song Contest winner, 'Puppet on A String', which sold four million copies world-wide. In 1968, she hosted her own TV series, but this

Lulu (above) 'jumps for joy' as the press release put it, on signing her *To Sir With Love* film contract. Sandie (left) looks altogether more relaxed

extra exposure did not stop Sandie Shaw's career from going on the rocks. However, like Lulu, she returned to the charts in the 1980s and 1990s. In 1984, when produced by her big fan, Morrissey, the pop princess not only re-appeared in the Top 20, but also amazingly topped the independent chart with 'Hand In Glove', and in 1993 she was featured on the hit charity single 'Gimme Shelter' - it seems that Sandie's bare feet are still very street credible.

MARIANNE FAITHFULL

Convent educated Marianne Faithfull (apparently her real name) is supposedly the daughter of an Austrian baroness. In 1964, her first hit, 'As Tears Go By', made the UK Top 10 and the US Top 30, a performance equalled on both sides of the Atlantic by her follow-up, 'Come And Stay With Me', a song written by Jackie De Shannon. This pattern continued with 'This Little Bird', written and originally recorded by John D. Loudermilk (her version easily outselling another British cover by the Nashville Teens), but after 'Summer Nights' (also in 1965), Faithfull's star began to wane, especially after she collapsed on stage in Morecambe during that summer, which necessitated cancellation of a projected US tour. Her relationship with Jagger ended after a drug overdose in 1969, while she was in Australia with the chief Rolling Stone when he was starring in the dubious feature film, *Ned Kelly*. After that, she retreated from the limelight to some extent until the late

Waif-like and vulnerable looking, Marianne Faithfull had male fans by the million after her 1964 debut on national television

1970s, when she re-emerged with a critically acclaimed album, and married punk rocker Ben Brierly (of The Vibrators). More recently, a 1989 album featured guest spots from such luminaries as Bono and Edge (of U2) and Steve Winwood.

The Star: Petula Clark's success transcended the Beat Boom into the league of the genuine International Celebrity

PETULA CLARK

Surrey-born Petula Clark released her debut disc in 1949, and first charted five years later, (there was no UK chart before the end of 1952) with 'The Little Shoemaker'. In 1957, her interpretation of Jodie Sands' beat ballad, 'With All My Heart', introduced the youthful veteran to rock record buyers, and her renditions of 'Alone' (originally by The Shepherd Sisters) and the hiccuppy 'Baby Lover' (first released by The Twin Tunes Quintet) kept her at the top. Clark's versions of the German hits, 'Sailor' and 'Romeo' returned her to the UK Top 5 in 1961, and in 1962 her bi-lingual twist treatment of Lee Dorsey's 'Ya Ya' was an Europe-wide winner. In 1964, her career took another upward turn when her recording of the anthemic discotheque record, 'Downtown', reached the runner-up spot in the UK, and went on to head the American charts. Clark followed this three million seller with such smash hits as 'I Know A Place', her second US No. 1, 'My Love', and the equally infectious transatlantic Top 10 entries, 'I Couldn't Live Without Your Love' and 'This Is My Song' (composed by Sir Charlie Chaplin). The singer, who has now celebrated 50 years in show business, has sold over 30 million records, and in 1988 increased her UK chart span to a record 34 years when a radically re-mixed version of her theme song, 'Downtown', zoomed into the Top 10.

In 1965 British girls Dodie West and Beryl Marsden reached the Top 30 with a cover of the Little Anthony & The Imperials classic, 'Goin' Out of My Head', and 'Who You Gonna Hurt', respectively, and in the following year, Genevieve briefly charted with 'Once'

Out of time

1966 THE BUBBLE BURSTS

Since the British Invasion forces first landed in the USA, it had become the rule for consistently successful UK hitmaking groups to score Stateside. Dave Dee, Dozy, Beaky, Mick & Titch, the first artists to crack the UK Top 20 in 1966, proved to be an exception to that rule. In total, this quaintly named quintet scored 11 successive British Top 20 hits (all penned by their managers, Ken Howard & Alan Blaikley), without ever cracking the US Top 40. Why that should have been is as much a mystery as why American Sixties superstars such as Paul Revere & The Raiders, Gary Lewis & The Playboys and Johnny Rivers never charted in Britain. Dave Dee and his motley crew recorded nothing but original material, and their records were often excellent examples of British pop at its best. Perhaps the reason they failed in the world's biggest record market was that the USA had recovered from the initial British invasion by the time they appeared, and was re-building its own formidable army of Beat Boom bands. Trend-setting British bands were still much in demand, but there was far less interest in importing basic pop artists, even such original contenders as Dave Dee, Dozy, Beaky, Mick & Titch.

Before January ended three more British groups popped up on the UK chart for the first time; The Overlanders, St. Louis Union and Pinkerton's Assorted Colours.

The Overlanders were no Johnny-come-latelys, having released their first single on Parlophone in 1961 as Pierce Rodgers & The Overlanders. In fact, *NME* had selected Rodgers (Laurie Mason) as one of the most promising artists of that year.

The Truth (above) had a minor hit with The Beatles' 'Girl', while David and Jonathan (right) smashed Stateside with 'Michelle'

The Castilles, who featured teenager Bruce Springsteen, released 'That's What You Get'

The Peter B's, who included later Fleetwood Mac members Mick Fleetwood & Peter Green, released an instrumental version of Jimmy Soul's US No.1, 'If You Wanna Be Happy', on Columbia

St.Louis Union (left) also scored with 'Girl', seen below in their moment of movie fame in *The Ghost Goes Gear*

However, even appearances on TV shows like, *Oh Boy!* did not push them chart-wards. The group, which then consisted of Mason (who was a winner on Carroll Levis' noted talent show when aged 12), Paul Arnold (real name Paul Friswell) and Peter Bartholomew signed to Pye in 1963. They released several folk-flavoured singles before their cover of 'Yesterday's Gone' gave them their first small smell of success. It reached the American Top 100, losing out to the original version by another British act, Chad & Jeremy. The group, which had now expanded to a quintet with the addition of bass and drums, had their only major British chart record with a timely cover of The Beatles' bilingual ballad, 'Michelle'. The Tony Hatch produced single took just three weeks to scale the summit. They were less fortunate Stateside, where again they lost a chart battle with a British duo; this time, David & Jonathan beat them to the punch.

SINGLE SUCCESS

Releasing as a single a cover version of a popular Beatles album track was almost like printing money in the mid-1960s. As soon as the Fab Four's Rubber Soul album bounced onto the street, record companies rushed their own artists into the studio to cover tracks. Apart from 'Michelle', another particularly popular song from that Beatles set was the plaintive 'Girl', which opened doors for two new UK acts, St. Louis Union and duo The Truth. The Manchester based sextet fronted by vocalist Tony Cassidy, were winners of a much publicised Beat Group Contest in *MM*. 'Girl' was not only their first release, but also their only passport to the chart. Before heading for one-hit wonderland, they made a fleeting appearance in the best-forgotten film, *The Ghost Goes Gear*.

The last of this particular trio of British one-hit heroes was Pinkerton's Assorted Colours, a visually distinctive outfit from Rugby, who were previously known by the punkish name The Liberators. Amplified autoharp player Sam 'Pinkerton' Kemp fronted the quintet, whose different coloured suits were the inspiration for their name. Pirate radio entrepreneur Reg Calvert managed their affairs, as he did

'Underground' newcomers Pink Floyd played their first major gig

for The Fortunes. Their debut single, 'Mirror Mirror', penned by guitarist Tony Newman, reached the British Top 10, but failed to break them in the States. The group, who for a while included Stuart Colman (Shakin' Stevens' future producer), later recorded with assorted names; Pinkerton's Colours and then simply as Pinkertons, but all to no avail. Belated success of a sort came their way in 1969, when they were recruited to become The Flying Machine. Under this name they were lucky enough to tour the US promoting the catchy, charmingly clichéd Top 10 hit 'Smile A Little Smile For Me', which a group of too-busy-to-leave-the-studio British session men had actually recorded.

TURNING POINT

The pop music scene had reached an important cross-roads by the spring and early summer of 1966. In Liverpool, the birth place of the Beat Boom, The Cavern Club had closed its doors, while in the USA, the pro-British pop show *Hullaballoo* had been junked and joined the other bastion of British Beat, *Shindig*, on the television scrap heap. There seemed little doubt that the trend-setting centre of the rock universe was moving from Britain to the West Coast of America.

California was fast becoming the main breeding ground for post-British Invasion bands; things were happening there in early 1966 that would change the shape of music on both sides of the Atlantic. The seeds of flower power were being sown on Haight Street in San Francisco, and the first crop of flower children

The *Swinging 66* tour, sponsored by pirate station Radio London, hit the road - its stars included The Small Faces, Crispian St. Peters and Wayne Fontana

Sam 'Pinkerton' Kemp (centre) with his autoharp, and (top) drummer David Holland and guitarist Tony Newman, (bottom) bassist Barrie Bernard and guitarist Tom Long

were starting to blossom. America's East Coast was also buzzing, with acts like Simon & Garfunkel finding international stardom, while less accessible artists, like the outrageous, obscure and sometimes obscene Fugs, tried to take their brand of underground music overground. In Britain, American artists Otis Redding, Wilson Pickett and James Brown were getting long overdue credit as soul music was hailed as the 'next big thing'. At the same time, Spanish group Los Bravos were belatedly proving with their huge transatlantic hit, 'Black Is Black', that other European countries could also participate in the Beat Boom. As an alternative to the commercial Beat Boom sounds, a trio of respected British musicians formed a blues/rock band appropriately called Cream, and signed with soul label Atlantic. The Beatles, too, had reached a turning point; John Lennon had made his infamous 'We're more popular than Jesus now' statement, and the group played their last live British show. An amazing array of musical styles was charting in the UK. Frank Sinatra was scoring his first ever transatlantic No. 1,

"If you liked or bought

The Troggs 'With A Girl Like You',

you may consider yourself the

lowest common denominator

in the pop audience"

Jonathan King

1966 TOP SINGLES IN THE UK

	TITLE	ARTIST
1	GREEN GREEN GRASS OF HOME	TOM JONES
2	DISTANT DRUMS	JIM REEVES
3	STRANGERS IN THE NIGHT	FRANK SINATRA
4	YELLOW SUBMARINE/ELEANOR RIGBY	THE BEATLES
5	THE SUN AIN'T GONNA SHINE (ANYMORE)	THE WALKER BROTHERS
6	REACH OUT I'LL BE THERE	THE FOUR TOPS
7	THESE BOOTS ARE MADE FOR WALKIN'	NANCY SINATRA
8	GOOD VIBRATIONS	THE BEACH BOYS
9	PRETTY FLAMINGO	MANFRED MANN
10	SUNNY AFTERNOON	THE KINKS
11	WITH A GIRL LIKE YOU	THE TROGGS
12	MICHELLE	THE OVERLANDERS
13	KEEP ON RUNNIN'	THE SPENCER DAVIS GROUP
14	SOMEBODY HELP ME	THE SPENCER DAVIS GROUP
15	PAPERBACK WRITER	THE BEATLES
16	YOU DON'T HAVE TO SAY YOU LOVE ME	DUSTY SPRINGFIELD
17	ALL OR NOTHING	THE SMALL FACES
18	OUT OF TIME	CHRIS FARLOWE
19	PAINT IT BLACK	THE ROLLING STONES
20	GET AWAY	GEORGIE FAME

Kilted Scotsman Kenneth McKellar represented Britain in the Eurovision Song Contest

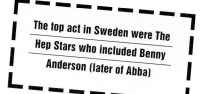

The top act in Sweden were The Hep Stars who included Benny Anderson (later of Abba)

1966
TOP SINGLES ARTISTS IN THE UK

1. **THE BEACH BOYS**
CAPITOL *US*

2. **THE SPENCER DAVIS GROUP**
FONTANA *UK*

3. **THE SMALL FACES**
DECCA *UK*

4. **THE KINKS**
PYE *UK*

5. **DAVE DEE, DOZY, BEAKY, MICK & TITCH** FONTANA *UK*

6. **THE TROGGS**
PAGE ONE *UK*

7. **THE ROLLING STONES**
DECCA *UK*

8. **THE HOLLIES**
PARLOPHONE *UK*

9. **THE WALKER BROTHERS**
PHILIPS *US*

10. **MANFRED MANN**
HMV *UK*

11. **THE BEATLES**
PARLOPHONE *UK*

12. **DUSTY SPRINGFIELD**
PHILIPS *UK*

13. **CILLA BLACK**
PARLOPHONE *UK*

14. **GENE PITNEY**
STATESIDE *US*

15. **THE SEEKERS**
COLUMBIA *UK*

16. **VAL DOONICAN**
DECCA *UK*

17. **TOM JONES**
DECCA *UK*

18. **CRISPIAN ST. PETERS**
DECCA *UK*

19. **THE WHO**
REACTION *UK*

20. **HERMAN'S HERMITS**
COLUMBIA *UK*

'Strangers In The Night', producer Phil Spector was hitting with his crowning glory, 'River Deep Mountain High' by Ike & Tina Turner (which cost him $22,000 to record), and the Beach Boys' 'God Only Knows' was also showing everyone (Beatles included) what could be achieved by spending months, instead of weeks, in the recording studio. Labels on both sides of the Atlantic were starting to actively seek out artists with album, rather than singles, sales potential. Ten years after rock had first altered the course of pop music, many of its performers were starting to take themselves and their music very seriously.

However, just when it looked as if basic good time beat bands might become an extinct species along came The Troggs, who, as their name suggests, appeared to have stepped out of the past. The quartet played a more raw and basic style of rock than the sophisticated mid-sixties' audience seemed to favour. They also looked decidedly dated in their garish striped suits and yesteryear hair styles, but, if anything those trappings added to their appeal. They became one of the biggest bands in Britain, and the only UK combo, apart from The Beatles and Rolling Stones, to top the American chart in 1966, which they did with their sexually suggestive second single, 'Wild Thing'. It appeared that a good dose of sex, Troggs and rock'n'roll was just what the doctor ordered for a vast number of record buyers,

"Rest assured that we shall never again return to the dark days of not so long ago, when the appearance of a British disc in the American charts was regarded as a fluke"
Derek Johnson, NME

who did not want their pop music too serious or subtle. Understandably, not everyone welcomed the brash and retrogressive band with open arms. For instance, the multi-faceted Jonathan King commented, 'if you liked or bought The Troggs 'With A Girl Like You', you may consider yourself the lowest common denominator in the pop audience.' Trogg Chris Britton responded, ' We never pretended our discs were educational or musically improving. They are simple uncluttered pieces of entertainment.' They may have been the butt of many musicians' jokes, but the West Country band, whose charismatic lead singer Ray Presley had few equals when it came to penning or performing suggestive lyrics, deservedly laughed all the way to the bank for several years.

The only other British group to make their transatlantic chart debut in 1966 were The New Vaudeville Band, whose formation was due solely to the runaway success of their single, 'Winchester Cathedral'. The idea for the dated ditty came from successful London-born composer Geoff Stephens, who was inspired to write it while staring at a photo of the ancient and impressive building. He visualised the record as being in the same novelty vein as early 1960s singles by The Temperance Seven, a humorous 1920/30s styled trad jazz band, who incidentally were producer George Martin's last big act before The Beatles. To ensure that he got exactly the vocal sound he wanted, Stephens sang the megaphoned lead himself. When 'Winchester Cathedral' became an instant hit a group was quickly formed to front it. This comic combo included vocalist Alan Klein, who tagged himself Tristram,

the Seventh Earl Of Cricklewood (a suburb in north London that would hardly merit an Earl), Henry Harrison (from the Rhythm & Blues group Cops 'N' Robbers, veterans of both the Pye and Decca labels) and Bob Kerr, who later, together with his entertaining 'Whoopee' Band, had his own UK TV series. The record not only reached the UK Top 5, but also topped the American charts, selling 1.5 million in just six weeks! It was also, somewhat amazingly, the recipient of the prestigious Grammy Award for Best Contemporary (Rock'n'Roll) Recording. The band's Winchester Cathedral album also climbed into the American Top 5 and passed the one million mark. Their next two similar sounding singles, Peek-A-Boo' written by Stephens & The Ivy League's John Carter, and 'Finchley Central', penned by Stephens and Klein (who had previously recorded as a solo singer for Oriole and Parlophone), both visited the UK Top 10 but neither made more than a small dent on the US Top 100. For the record, The New Vaudeville Band were still playing

The headliners at the National Jazz & Blues Festival at Windsor included The Who (whose fans rioted), The Yardbirds, The Move, Georgie Fame and The Small Faces

The New Vaudeville Band posing (above) and (left) seeing how many English eccentrics can fit into two American telephone booths

1966
TOP SINGLES ARTISTS IN THE US

"American pop will force its British counterpart into the back seat within a year"

Sid Bernstein

the cabaret and club circuit on both sides of the Atlantic long after the Beat Boom was a distant memory. By the autumn of 1966, many people on both sides of the water believed the Beat Boom bubble had now burst and it would soon be history. When noted North of England music journalist Bill Harry was asked by an A&R man which Manchester groups were worth a visit, he was taken aback when he realised he could not think of any worthy of recommendation. This was a sure sign to him that the flood of talent from Britain's second Beat City was drying up. At the same time, much to his surprise, top EMI A&R man Peter Eden came back from an exhaustive scouting trip of Liverpool and Manchester completely empty handed. The astute *NME* journalist Derek Johnson also wondered whether the big British Beat Boom was over. He had noticed that for the first time in nearly four and a half years there were more American records on the UK chart than British (albeit many of them on the lower rungs), and that sales of UK records in America and other parts of the world were dropping. He also noted that The Beatles' last American tour had been less successful than the previous two, while reporting that US entrepreneur Sid Bernstein, who had promoted The Beatles at Shea Stadium, had commented 'American pop will force its British counterpart into the back seat within a year.' Johnson opined that the position was not as black as it might appear, pointing out that UK acts had maintained a pretty firm foothold in the US, and that many of the successful groups in other parts of the world had simply learned the tricks of the trade from British bands. 'This' he said 'does not alter the fact that British groups are still the masters and are acknowledged as such.' He summed up the whole situation thus; 'The initial fever pitch of excitement has now, inevitably, subsided. British performers have found a level in the world of pop – and a very high level it is too. What's more' he added prophetically 'it's a level we can maintain indefinitely.' He concluded 'Whatever happens, Britain has made her mark upon the world of pop. After years of playing second fiddle, America now accepts us as a force to be reckoned with. We've arrived on the world market and we're there to stay. There will be ups and downs - but rest assured that we shall never again return to the dark days of not so long ago, when the appearance of a British disc in the American charts was regarded as a fluke.'

A glance at the final American Top 20 singles chart of the year showed only two UK acts in residence, and neither of these a beat group. On the other hand, there were 10 US groups present, including the No.1, The Monkees, whose top rated television series was very successfully launched in Britain on the last day of 1966.

In the UK, sales of singles were down again (they had dropped 15% the previous year), this time by 17%. These figures were disappointing, but LP sales had increased by 6% (after a rise of 13% the previous year), and the $60 million earned by recorded music was more than double the amount taken in 1959.

From a British standpoint, by the last quarter of the year things looked ominous, indicating that US artists had made a very strong comeback after three years of UK domination. American acts led in most categories; Jim Reeves was Top Male Artist, Top Album Artist, and his 'Distant Drums' the Top Single. The soundtrack LP The Sound Of Music was the Top Album, and even in the group sections, where home-grown combos had previously been unassailable, American acts ruled; The Beach Boys were Top Album Act and The Four Tops headed the Top Singles Groups. The last quarter's top three producers were also all American: Shel Talmy, Holland, Dozier & Holland and Chet Atkins. In fact Dusty Springfield, the Top Female Singles artist, was the only British act to head a category.

DAVE DEE, DOZY, BEAKY, MICK AND TICH

This colourful pop/rock group were formed in Salisbury, Wiltshire, as Dave Dee & The Bostons (named after the popular haircut of the period). Apart from vocalist

The only British artists to reach the American Top 10 were the Beatles, The Dave Clark Five, The Animals, The Kinks, The Rolling Stones and The New Vaudeville Band

The Monkees (opposite) were the teenybop sensation of the year worldwide, as were, in Great Britain, Dave Dee, Dozy, Beaky, Mick and Tich

Dee (born Dave Harman), the quintet's line-up was: Trevor 'Dozy' Davies (bass), John 'Beaky' Dymond (guitar), Mick Wilson (drums) and Ian 'Tich' Amey (lead guitar). They were spotted by The Honeycombs' managers and songwriters, Ken Howard and Alan Blaikley, after they had honed their humour-laced act in both Hamburg and various local clubs. Howard & Blaikley gave them their far more distinctive name and signed them to Fontana Records. The band's third release, the thumping 'You Make It Move', moved into the Top 20 in early 1966 and then hit followed hit for the flashily fashionable fivesome. In 1966, they spent more weeks in the UK singles chart than any other act. Among the band's best remembered 45s are the anthemic 'Hold Tight', the foot-stomping, gibberish gem 'Zabadak' (their only US Top 100 entry), the lyrically suspect 'Bend It' (banned in several territories) and the whip-cracking 'Legend Of Xanadu', which topped some charts. American Steve Rowland produced their singles, which almost always contained interesting ideas and instrumentation, left-field lyrics and ear-catching sounds. Nevertheless, by 1969 ardour among British teenagers for the theatrical outfit was abating, and Dee decided to move on, becoming a well-respected A&R executive in the 1970s, while the group – tagging themselves Dozy, Beaky Mick and Tich – regularly re-worked their hits on the 'oldies' circuit.

John's Children (who were soon to be joined by Decca artist Marc Bolan) released a debut single on Columbia

1966 TOP SINGLES IN THE US

	TITLE	ARTIST
1	I'M A BELIEVER	THE MONKEES
2	WINCHESTER CATHEDRAL	THE NEW VAUDEVILLE BAND
3	(YOU'RE MY) SOUL & INSPIRATION	THE RIGHTEOUS BROTHERS
4	WE CAN WORK IT OUT	THE BEATLES
5	GOOD VIBRATIONS	THE BEACH BOYS
6	MONDAY MONDAY	THE MAMAS & THE PAPAS
7	SUMMER IN THE CITY	THE LOVIN' SPOONFUL
8	CHERISH	THE ASSOCIATION
9	WILD THING	THE TROGGS
10	YOU CAN'T HURRY LOVE	THE SUPREMES
11	REACH OUT I'LL BE THERE	THE FOUR TOPS
12	96 TEARS	? (QUESTION MARK) & THE MYSTERIANS
13	THE BALLAD OF THE GREEN BERETS	SSGT. BARRY SADLER
14	PAINT IT BLACK	THE ROLLING STONES
15	LAST TRAIN TO CLARKSVILLE	THE MONKEES
16	YOU KEEP ME HANGIN' ON	THE SUPREMES
17	WHEN A MAN LOVES A WOMAN	PERCY SLEDGE
18	HANKY PANKY	TOMMY JAMES & THE SHONDELLS
19	MY LOVE	PETULA CLARK
20	THE SOUND OF SILENCE	SIMON & GARFUNKEL

TROGGS

This band from Andover, Hampshire, started life as The Troglodytes, a name that was shortened to The Troggs after ex-Ten Feet Five members, Chris Britton (guitar) and Pete Staples (bass) joined Ronnie Bond (drums) and vocalist Reg Presley (real name Reg Ball) in the quartet's line-up. They signed up with The Kinks' manager, Larry Page, who placed them with Fontana after CBS Records lost their 1966 debut single, 'Lost Girl'. Their next release, a cover of 'Wild Thing', a song originally recorded by New York discotheque band Jordan Christopher & The Wild Ones, was an instant hit, reaching No. 2 in the UK and going one better in America (where, due to legal problems, it was released on two labels). Over the next few months, The Troggs had two UK Top 10 albums and returned to the British Top 10 with the similarly basic singles, 'With A Girl Like You' (which reached No. 1), 'I Can't Control Myself' and 'Any Way You Want Me'. The former two came from Reg Presley's pen and the latter was specially written for them by 'Wild Thing' composer Chip Taylor. After a relatively quiet period, The Troggs re-appeared in the Transatlantic Top 10 in 1968 with another Presley pop pearl, 'Love Is All Around'. In future years, The Troggs were no strangers to the nostalgia bandwagon, and Presley, who placed his tongue more firmly in his cheek as the years went by, joined the short-lived 1989 Sixties-revival act, The Travelin' Wrinklies. In the 1990s The Troggs recorded with long-time fans REM in Georgia. Bond, whose drumming was discussed on the infamous 'Troggs Tapes', (a now-legendary bootleg recording, made when an engineer left a studio recorder running and taped the band having a violent argument) died in 1992.

I'M BACKING BRITAIN

1963-66 TOP SINGLES IN THE UK

	TITLE	ARTIST
1	SHE LOVES YOU	THE BEATLES
2	TEARS	KEN DODD
3	GREEN GREEN GRASS OF HOME	TOM JONES
4	FROM ME TO YOU	THE BEATLES
5	DISTANT DRUMS	JIM REEVES
6	I WANT TO HOLD YOUR HAND	THE BEATLES
7	DAY TRIPPER/WE CAN WORK IT OUT	THE BEATLES
8	I FEEL FINE	THE BEATLES
9	I LIKE IT	GERRY & THE PACEMAKERS
10	THE CARNIVAL IS OVER	THE SEEKERS
11	STRANGERS IN THE NIGHT	FRANK SINATRA
12	DO YOU LOVE ME	BRIAN POOLE & THE TREMELOES
13	YOU'LL NEVER WALK ALONE	GERRY & THE PACEMAKERS
14	GLAD ALL OVER	THE DAVE CLARK FIVE
15	DIAMONDS	JET HARRIS & TONY MEEHAN
16	YOU'RE MY WORLD	CILLA BLACK
17	IT'S OVER	ROY ORBISON
18	YELLOW SUBMARINE/ELEANOR RIGBY	THE BEATLES
19	HOW DO YOU DO IT?	GERRY & THE PACEMAKERS
20	CONFESSIN'	FRANK IFIELD

1963-66
TOP UK RECORDING ARTISTS

1	**THE BEATLES**	PARLOPHONE *UK*
2	**CLIFF RICHARD**	COLUMBIA *UK*
3	**THE ROLLING STONES**	DECCA *UK*
4	**THE HOLLIES**	PARLOPHONE *UK*
5	**MANFRED MANN**	HMV *UK*
6	**ROY ORBISON**	LONDON AMERICAN *US*
7	**THE KINKS**	PYE *UK*
8	**THE SEARCHERS**	PYE *UK*
9	**ELVIS PRESLEY**	RCA *US*
10	**THE SHADOWS**	COLUMBIA *UK*
11	**GENE PITNEY**	UA *US*
12	**THE BACHELORS**	DECCA *UK*
13	**CILLA BLACK**	PARLOPHONE *UK*
14	**GERRY & THE PACEMAKERS**	COLUMBIA *UK*
15	**THE ANIMALS**	COLUMBIA *UK*
16	**DUSTY SPRINGFIELD**	PHILIPS *UK*
17	**JIM REEVES**	RCA *US*
18	**SANDIE SHAW**	PYE *UK*
19	**THE SEEKERS**	COLUMBIA *AUSTRALIA*
20	**BILLY J. KRAMER & THE DAKOTAS**	PARLOPHONE *UK*

1963-66
TOP GROUPS IN THE UK

1. **THE BEATLES**
   PARLOPHONE *UK*
2. **THE ROLLING STONES**
   DECCA *UK*
3. **THE HOLLIES**
   PARLOPHONE *UK*
4. **MANFRED MANN**
   HMV *UK*
5. **THE KINKS**
   PYE *UK*
6. **THE SEARCHERS**
   PYE *UK*
7. **THE SHADOWS**
   COLUMBIA *UK*
8. **THE BACHELORS**
   DECCA *UK*
9. **GERRY & THE PACEMAKERS**
   COLUMBIA *UK*
10. **THE ANIMALS**
    COLUMBIA *UK*
11. **THE SEEKERS**
    COLUMBIA *Australia*
12. **BILLY J. KRAMER & THE DAKOTAS**
    PARLOPHONE *UK*
13. **HERMAN'S HERMITS**
    COLUMBIA *UK*
14. **THE BEACH BOYS**
    CAPITOL *US*
15. **THE SUPREMES**
    TAMLA MOTOWN *US*
16. **FREDDIE & THE DREAMERS**
    COLUMBIA *UK*
17. **THE WALKER BROTHERS**
    PHILIPS *US*
18. **BRIAN POOLE & THE TREMELOES**
    DECCA *UK*
19. **THE YARDBIRDS**
    COLUMBIA *UK*
20. **THE DAVE CLARK FIVE**
    COLUMBIA *UK*

1963-66
TOP MALE ARTISTS IN THE UK

1. **CLIFF RICHARD**
   COLUMBIA *UK*
2. **ROY ORBISON**
   LONDON AMERICAN *US*
3. **ELVIS PRESLEY**
   RCA *US*
4. **GENE PITNEY**
   UA *US*
5. **JIM REEVES**
   RCA *US*
6. **BILLY FURY**
   DECCA *UK*
7. **FRANK IFIELD**
   COLUMBIA *UK*
8. **TOM JONES**
   DECCA *UK*
9. **KEN DODD**
   COLUMBIA *UK*
10. **BOB DYLAN**
    CBS *US*
11. **P.J. PROBY**
    LIBERTY *US*
12. **VAL DOONICAN**
    DECCA *UK*
13. **DEL SHANNON**
    LONDON AMERICAN *US*
14. **GEORGIE FAME**
    COLUMBIA *UK*
15. **DAVE BERRY**
    DECCA *UK*
16. **DONOVAN**
    PYE *UK*
17. **BUDDY HOLLY**
    CORAL *US*
18. **ANDY WILLIAMS**
    CBS *US*
19. **CRISPIAN ST. PETERS**
    DECCA *UK*
20. **ADAM FAITH**
    PARLOPHONE *UK*

1963-66
TOP FEMALE ARTISTS IN THE UK

1. **CILLA BLACK**
   PARLOPHONE *UK*
2. **DUSTY SPRINGFIELD**
   PHILIPS *UK*
3. **SANDY SHAW**
   PYE *UK*
4. **PETULA CLARK**
   PYE *UK*
5. **MARIANNE FAITHFULL**
   DECCA *UK*
6. **BRENDA LEE**
   BRUNSWICK *US*
7. **KATHY KIRBY**
   DECCA *UK*
8. **CHER**
   LIBERTY *US*
9. **NANCY SINATRA**
   REPRISE *US*
10. **LULU**
    DECCA *UK*
11. **JACKIE TRENT**
    PYE *UK*
12. **MILLIE**
    FONTANA *UK*
13. **JULIE ROGERS**
    MERCURY *UK*
14. **TWINKLE**
    DECCA *UK*
15. **DIONNE WARWICK**
    PYE INT. *US*
16. **MARY WELLS**
    STATESIDE *US*
17. **SHIRLEY BASSEY**
    COLUMBIA *UK*
18. **SHIRLEY ELLIS**
    LONDON AMERICAN *US*
19. **LESLEY GORE**
    MERCURY *US*
20. **THE SINGING NUN**
    PHILIPS *Belgium*

I'm A Man

MALE SOLOISTS

Cliff Richard was the most successful solo name in British rock, though closely associated with his backing group The Shadows, both to be usurped for a time by the Beat Boom groups

The Beat Boom did no favours for British solo male vocalists. Almost overnight, groups made the idea of a solo singer seem almost redundant. Despite this, three famous examples of this almost extinct breed still found themselves among the Top 10 artists of 1963: Cliff Richard, Frank Ifield and Billy Fury continued to add to their impressive Top 20 tallies. In fact, Cliff ended the year second only to The Beatles, although some credit for his success should go to his backing group, The Shadows. It was the year that early 1960s No. 1 hit makers, Frankie Vaughan and singer/actor John Leyton, enjoyed their final days as major chart forces. It was also the time that clean-cut teen balladeer Mark Wynter and talents like Joe Brown, Karl Denver, Buddy Holly-inspired vocalist Mike Berry (who returned to the Top 20 in 1980) and Kenny Lynch, also fired their last significant chart bound shots, and veteran MOR merchants, Jimmy Young (now a BBC radio presenter) and Ronnie Carroll, said farewell to the sharp end of the chart.

Traditional jazz also had its final fling, with mid-chart entries from Kenny Ball & His Jazzmen and Acker Bilk and his Paramount Jazz Band. Fellow British instrumentalists John Barry and Ken Thorne (and their Orchestras) also made solitary appearances in the Top 20 in 1963. Meanwhile, on the album front, only Cliff Richard, Frank Ifield, Billy Fury, trumpeter Ball and singer/actor Anthony Newley reached the UK Top 10, with MOR stalwart Mantovani & His Orchestra alone managing an American Top 10 album placing.

HOGGING THE HEADLINES

Groups hogged the hit parade so much in 1963 that the only British male soloists to make their Top 20 debuts in that auspicious year were ex-Tornados' bass player, Heinz, and the unique Dave Berry. Heinz, who left the transatlantic chart topping Tornados in spring, 1963, had his only Top 10 entry with his second single, 'Just Like Eddie'. He said about this tribute to Eddie Cochran, 'I've nothing against Buddy Holly, but I think Eddie Cochran should be more recognised. It's about time someone paid homage to one of the great rock entertainers. People ape Eddie just like they do Buddy, but this seems to go unrecognised.' His heartfelt performance gave the photogenic performer, with the teutonic good looks and striking blonde hair, the first of five Top 30 entries, and proved once again the pop truism that a great voice is not essential for a hit record maker.

Dave Berry may have had most of his success with cover records, but this should not detract from the fact that he was one of the most original British performers of the rock era. His stage act was unique - something one could not say about many of his compatriots. He performed his songs accompanied by tongue-in-cheek, semi-erotic body movements, and his act relied heavily on playing peek-a-boo with the audience, either with his turned up coat collar or through his ever mobile fingers. Berry managed to get a

Last of the old wave, first of the new: Heinz (left) was part of the pre-Beat pop that was being overtaken by the likes of the enigmatic Dave Berry (below)

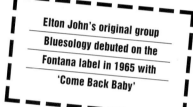

Elton John's original group Bluesology debuted on the Fontana label in 1965 with 'Come Back Baby'

more frenzied reaction from girls by just letting his fingers do the walking (often simply caressing his mike lead or any other handy prop) than far more blatantly sexual performers achieved by using their whole bodies. When asked how he came up with his style of stage presentation he said, 'It all started in a small club in Sheffield, which was so packed that nobody could move, least of all me, and I had to perform. I couldn't just stand there and sing so I started this coat movement on the spot. The audience loved it, I'm very happy to say.' Berry's first single was a cover of 'Memphis Tennessee', a song written and first recorded by one of his musical heroes, Chuck Berry. It took almost nine hours to record due to the lack of studio experience of his backing band, The Cruisers. After that single, session men were used to back him on his records (these sometimes included guitarist Jimmy Page and bass player John Paul Jones - later Led Zeppelin members). Berry, who clocked up one UK Top 20 single every year between 1963-1966, is best known for his haunting 1964 recording of 'The Crying Game', which featured outstanding guitar work from Big Jim Sullivan

C&W singer Houston Wells reached the lower rungs of the Top 30 with his treatment of 'Only The Heartaches', penned by Nashville writer Wayne P. Walker who had previously composed hits for Andy Williams, Johnny Burnette and Eddie Cochran. Mike

Part of the mainstream of British showbiz, Benny Hill (above) and Val Doonican made their chart appearances despite the rock revolution going on around them

Cotton & His Jazzmen also had a minor hit with their trad adaptation of the spiritual, 'Swing That Hammer' as did Don Spencer with the theme from Gerry Anderson's puppet TV show, *Fireball XL5*. Ex-Most Brother, Mickie Most - whom publicity agents assured the public had scored 11 No. 1 hits in South Africa (a fact that charts do not back up) - also reached the Top 30 with 'Mr. Porter'. Shortly afterwards, Most (who at the time worked alongside this author in a Soho disco) produced The Animals, and, as they say, the rest is musical history. Although, they were no newcomers, both comedian/singer Harry Secombe and Benny Hill also had singles in the last third of the Top 30. Secombe, who had initially found fame in radio's *The Goon Show*, scored with the big ballad, 'If I Ruled The World'. The humorous novelty 'Harvest Of Love' gave Hill, who later became one of the most popular British funny men ever in the States, his third UK hit.

KEEPING THE FLAG FLYING

In 1963, the only UK male singer to make any kind of impact in America was Cliff Richard, who appeared on the Ed Sullivan show (alongside fellow countryman Frank Ifield), and whose update of 'It's All In The Game' cracked the Top 40 as the year ended. It was a year when Cliff was not only voted Most Promising Male Singer in the prestigious American teen magazine, *16*, but also took the crown from Elvis Presley in the World's Top Male Singer category in the *NME* poll. Incidentally, Presley, who continued his unprecedented British chart run, was joined in the year's Top 20 artists by fellow US males Roy Orbison, Del Shannon and the late Buddy Holly - only half the number listed the previous year.

The Beat Boom did not affect the standing of US male vocalists in the UK, and 1964's Top 20 Artists again included a quartet of them, with Jim Reeves (who died that year) and Gene Pitney lining up with the omnipresent Elvis Presley and the 'Big O' – Roy Orbison. However, in the same year that British groups forced the United Kingdom into the American musical arena, the only local male to make the year's Top 20 acts was Cliff Richard at No. 12. In Britain, it was the year that Adam Faith, Eden Kane and yodelling pop star Frank Ifield bid adieu to the Top 20, and when Cliff Bennett, Val Doonican and soap opera personality Chris Sandford made their chart debuts. 1964 was also the year that balladeer Matt Monro, Billy Fury and, of course, Cliff Richard (who recorded in America for the first time that year) helped keep the flag flying for lone male vocalists.

Cliff Bennett, whose first single had surfaced in 1961, was one of best basic rock'n'roll singers Britain ever produced. The relative failure of his excellent debut releases forced him to join similar styled retro-rockers in the cellar clubs of Hamburg, where they still appreciated real rock'n'roll. With his backing band, The Rebel Rousers (named after Duane Eddy's 1958 hit), Bennett deservedly scored two big British hits in the mid-1960s, 'One Way Love' and 'Got To Get You Into My Life'. The former was a mid-table American hit for The Drifters, and the latter song was taken from an album by his ex- Hamburg honchos, The Beatles.

Val Doonican, a casually dressed pleasant-voiced MOR singer, was, in his own unassuming way, one of Britain's top artists in the 1960s. He was also one of only three UK males to reach the Top 10 album chart in 1964 (the others being Frank Ifield and Cliff Richard). Doonican first came to the British public's attention when his rendition of the bouncy 'Walk Tall' (later a US country hit for Faron Young) went into the Top 3. This Irish singer, who frequently foraged through the Nashville song book, went on to clock up eight Top 20 singles and five Top 20 albums. Actor/singer Chris Sandford also briefly joined the exclusive Top 20 club in 1964. Johnny Worth, who had previously written chart toppers for Adam Faith and Eden Kane, penned Sandford's sole success, 'Not Too Little Not Too Much'. Ex-skiffler Sandford, who was backed by his group The Coronets, later recorded unsuccessfully with The Rag N Bone Band, and as Chris Sandford's Friendship (under which name he covered The Doobie Brothers 'Listen To The Music'). Sandford, who played the gormless, though likeable, window cleaner Wally Potts in the top rated TV soap opera *Coronation Street*, was never to climb any further up the ladder of pop fame.

Two Liverpool lads, Tony Jackson and Tommy Quickly, narrowly missed the Top 20 that year. Jackson, who had been a vocalist with the chart-topping Searchers, charted with a Mersey-styled update of Mary Wells' 1961 American debut hit, 'Bye Bye Baby', on which he was backed by his new band, The Vibrations. Tommy Quickly was the first male solo artist managed by Brian Epstein, and as such received the full promotional push on his 1963 debut disc, the Lennon & McCartney composition 'Tip Of My Tongue'. Although this single disappeared without reaching the chart, Quickly's next few releases also received plenty of publicity, and his revival of the country standard, 'Wild Side Of Life' was his passport to one-hit wonderland . Drummer Tony Meehan, who had previously tasted success with The Shadows and in partnership with Jet Harris, also only achieved one minor hit in his own right; 'Song Of Mexico'.

America may have gone overboard for British groups, and been infatuated by UK female singers in 1964, but the only British male soloists to make any noticeable noise were Sinatra sound-alike Matt Monro and Danny Williams, a singer in the Johnny Mathis mould.

THE HIP HOPES

Monro (born Terence Parsons), was a one-time London bus driver who had made his disc debut on Decca in 1956. The singer, whom George Martin recorded in the late 1950s as Fred Flange, had his first notable UK hit in 1961 with 'Portrait Of My Love', his recording of this timeless ballad (covered successfully in America by Steve Lawrence) being voted Record of The Year by *MM* readers. Later in 1961, Monro's interpretation of another classy British MOR song, 'My Kind Of Girl', quickly conveyed him into the Top 5 in his homeland and lifted him into the US Top 20. It was also responsible for his being voted not only Top International Act, but also Most Promising Male Singer in *Billboard* magazine's 1961 DJ poll. In the following year, Monro had a big British hit with the original version of the

> Screen actor and later TV and musical star Michael Crawford had a 1965 single release on the United Artists label

Matt Monro, another untypical star of the mid-Sixties, in action here at the smart London night club Talk Of The Town

plaintive 'Softly As I Leave You' (later associated with Elvis Presley). His last American success came in 1964 when his third British Top 5 single, 'Walk Away', narrowly missed the US Top 20. Incidentally, it was Monro, rather than The Beatles, who had the biggest British single hit in the 1960s with Lennon & McCartney's classic lost love lament, 'Yesterday'.

South African born, ultra-smooth song stylist Danny Williams was recruited to HMV in 1959 by producer/songwriter Norman Newell. Like Adam Faith, the velvet voiced vocalist was a regular on BBC TV's 1959 pop show, *Drumbeat*. In the early 1960s, Williams had three British Top 20 successes, 'Jeannie' (co-written by top UK pianist Russ Conway), 'Wonderful World Of The Young' (a ballad previously recorded by Andy Williams), and a chart topping version of the memorable 'Moon River', a song again associated with Andy Williams, but one which had actually been a bigger US singles hit for both composer Henry Mancini and R&B vocalist Jerry Butler. Surprisingly, his sojourn in the American Top 10 came after he had joined the so-called 'too good for the chart' brigade in his adopted homeland. The song that briefly made him a Stateside celebrity in 1964 was an American composition, 'White On White'. Even though Williams impressed many people on his three-week US promotional tour in 1964, his subsequent Stateside singles stiffed.

The only other UK males even to grace the lower rungs of the US Top 100 that year, were Beatles' producer George Martin (& His Orchestra) and Bobby Shafto. Martin's sole single success as an artist came with an instrumental interpretation of

Danny Williams (above) who's 'Moon River' originally featured in the Audrey Hepburn movie *Breakfast At Tiffany's*

"I've been getting in a rut. I need a hit record now, so I can speak to a bigger audience."

Georgie Fame

the lilting Beatles' ballad, 'This Boy', which he released under the title 'Ringo's Theme' (his version being featured in The Beatles debut film *A Hard Day's Night*). Shafto was one of the few British acts who found more fame on the other side of the Atlantic. The lowly Top 100 placing of his single, 'She's My Girl' (penned by Peter Callander and Len Beadle), hardly made him a Stateside star, but it was a better result than he achieved with any of his eight UK releases on Parlophone.

It was a much different story in 1965, when Georgie Fame, Tom Jones, Donovan and Jonathan King made their first transatlantic chart indents.

Georgie Fame, who at 16 joined Larry Parnes' well-known stable of artists, was one of the first performers on the live British R&B scene. When asked the old question about whether a white man could sing the blues, he was adamant 'many of us are capable of feeling and singing the blues.' His debut single, which coupled 'Do The Dog' (originally by Rufus Thomas) and 'Shop Around' (the first major US hit for The Miracles), almost made the grade, as did several subsequent sides. In late 1964, Fame admitted 'I've been getting in a rut. I need a hit record now, so I can speak out to a bigger audience.' Although he did not initially realise its potential, the song that was to make him famous was 'Yeh Yeh', a Lambert, Hendricks &

Initially fronting a backing group, The Squires, Tom Jones proved to be one of the most enduring UK names from the Beat era

"I love Tom Jones' style. He's a real singer."

Nat 'King' Cole

Ross track, which singer Elkie Brooks had brought to his attention. Fame originally intended recording 'Yeh Yeh' solely for members of his fan club, considering it too jazz based and not young-sounding enough to be a hit, but it pushed the right buttons with the record buying public and shot to the top of the British chart. In his career, this talented performer, whose style resembles that of the American jazz singer/keyboard player Mose Allison, amassed eight UK Top 20 singles and four Top 20 albums. Proof of his popularity came in 1965, when he was added to a star-studded Motown package tour (which included The Supremes, The Temptations, The Miracles, Stevie Wonder and Martha & The Vandellas), which was surprisingly only attracting small advance ticket sales. His name not only helped pull the punters, but he was also received as warmly as any of the Detroit R&B deities.

JONES THE VOICE

The new British male vocalist who caused the most impact in 1965 was Tom Jones, whose earliest recordings with hit producer Joe Meek in 1963 were not even deemed good enough to release at the time. Jones joined Decca the following year, and the label launched him with an exciting interpretation of Ronnie Love's 'Chills & Fever', which critically well received but failed to chart. He started his winning streak in 1965 with 'It's Not Unusual', an unusually uplifting song originally written for Sandie Shaw by Jones' manager, ex-Viscount Gordon Mills. America instantly fell for the Jones boy, and he spent much of 1965 in the States, appearing on TV (sometimes filmed only from the waist up – as was earlier hip-shaker Elvis Presley in 1956) and on stage, in shows hosted by top DJs Murray The K. and Dick Clark. Few artists could keep up with Jones during that year - he had a quartet of big British hits and saw five of his singles climb into the top half of the US chart,

including the 1963 Meek-produced 'Little Lonely One' (based on 'Santa Lucia'), first recorded by The Jarmels. Jones' appeal crossed age, sex and racial barriers. Dionne Warwick told him 'I couldn't believe you were white', and Motown's Mary Wells commented 'I never thought I'd hear a white man sing like that', a remark that pleased him. 'I'm glad I sound like that, because I love R&B' Jones said, and clarified the statement by saying 'I don't mean what they call R&B in Britain, I mean the real thing.' It was no surprise when he walked away with the Grammy for Best New Artist of the year. It appeared that many people agreed with legendary entertainer Nat 'King' Cole when he said 'I love Tom Jones' style. He's a real singer.'

By no stretch of the imagination could one describe Donovan as a darling of the cabaret circuit, but this hippies' hero was one of the most important, influential and consistent hit making British males of the 1960s. Fame came quickly for the Glasgow born singer/songwriter, after his shrewd production and management team, Peter Eden and noted composer Geoff Stephens, convinced the top rated TV show, *Ready Steady Go*, to book him for for an unprecedented three successive weeks (they actually had an option on a further six consecutive weeks, which, by an oversight, they forgot to take up). Donovan's Dylanesque appearance and style caused instant controversy, and the phoney folk feud between them helped hurl his debut single, 'Catch The Wind', into the British Top 10 (it entered the Top 30 a week before Dylan's debut on that chart with 'Times They Are A-Changin' '). The supposed rivalry between Bob Dylan and Donovan certainly did neither act any harm, and both went on to far greater things. Within a few months of turning professional, Donovan was appearing on the bill with Dylan at the prestigious Newport Folk Festival, and soon afterwards picked up the trophy for Top Newcomer in the *NME* poll. He went on from being the sterotype folk-rocker to the archetypal flower-child; his career blossomed throughout the late 1960s, resulting in a bunch of hit singles and albums, but, it was wilting by the time of Woodstock in 1969. Return visits to his mentor Eden in the early 1970s, and producer Mickie Most later that decade, both failed to increase his enviable crop of hits - he might as well have tried to catch the wind.

"I know my voice doesn't sound too clear, but then I don't think I've got much of a voice."

Jonathan King

OPINIONATED

Another of the new British male artists who joined relative veterans Billy Fury, Matt Monro, comedian turned singer Ken Dodd, and, of course, Cliff Richard on the UK charts in 1965, was Jonathan King, an opinionated writer/producer/singer and talent-spotter extrordinaire. His first venture in the music business was as producer of Terry Ward & The Bumblies' little remembered single, 'Gotta Tell', on Fontana. The never-so-humble King had much better luck with his own debut, 'Everyone's Gone To The Moon', which went to No. 3 in Britain and into the US Top 20. When asked about the song's origin, King confided that it started out as a take-off of Bob Dylan, whom the ex-Cambridge student considered 'used a lot of adolescent truisms in his songs.' King said of the record, 'The lyrics meant something to some people - though not me', adding 'I particularly like the vague, wistful, airy-fairy recorded sound', he concluded 'I know my voice doesn't sound too clear, but then I don't think I've got much of a voice.' It was to be his only chart record as a vocalist in the 1960s. However, before the decade closed, King, with his producer/writer's hat on, hit with 'It's Good News Week' by Hedgehoppers Anonymous, and introduced a largely uninterested world to his discoveries Genesis. Before the end of the Swinging Sixties, the multi-faceted King also hosted his own TV chat show and wrote a well-read column in *Disc*. In the following decade, he was almost as successful as he thought he deserved to be, scoring with a string of British successes released under a plethora of names.

YESTERDAY'S MEN

Chris Andrews and Ian Whitcomb were two other British singer/songwriters who had giant hits in 1965. Chris Andrews, like many of his peers, was a veteran of the German club scene, and released his debut disc, 'I Do', under the name Chris Ravel & The Ravers on Decca in 1963. Only months after this single failed to do the trick, Andrews charted for the first time as composer of Adam Faith's aptly titled 'The First Time'. Faith then recorded a string of songs penned by the singer/songwriter from Essex, and when his protégée Sandie Shaw sought strong original material, Andrews was the obvious person to supply it. He wrote the vast majority of Shaw's best known singles, including the incontestably commercial Top 10 entries, 'Girl Don't Come', 'I'll Stop At Nothing', 'Message Understood' and the chart topping 'Long Live Love'. Encouraged by this success, Andrews returned to singing, and his self-composed, sing-a-long pop stomper, 'Yesterday Man', held the runner-up slot for three weeks in late 1965, and went on to top the German chart, breach the US Top 100, and sell over a million copies world-wide. His subsequent Decca releases, 'To Whom It Concerns' and 'Something On My Mind', also made the British Top 30. However, by the end of 1966, the runner-up to Most Promising New Artist in the *NME* poll, was indeed yesterday's man.

During his studies at Dublin's Trinity College, Surrey-born Ian Whitcomb fronted the R&B band Bluesville. The group's haunting Animals-styled interpretation of the folk favourite, 'This Sporting Life', made a minor dent on the US Top 100 in 1965. For his next release, Whitcomb's American label, the Capitol subsidiary Tower, selected the radically different but self-composed 'You Turn Me On' – a track Whitcomb regarded as junk. This few-holds-barred rock-rooted record came complete with a stammering high-pitched vocal and wild Jerry Lee Lewis-like piano pounding. The result may have turned off record buyers in his homeland, but it had the opposite effect in

> Steve Gibbons first recorded with Birmingham group The Uglys, with 'Wake Up My Mind' on the Pye label

Three faces of Sixties pop: the intuitive Donovan (above opposite), opportunist King (below opposite) and straight professional Chris Andrews (left)

America, where, despite being banned by some stations, this fun 45 turned up in the Top 10. Whitcomb's follow-up, another rockin' novelty, 'N-E-R-V-O-U-S', climbed halfway up the US chart, but, after that he seemed to lose visitation rights to the chart. Whitcomb, who is an authority on the history of popular music, wrote the successful books *After The Ball* and *Whole Lotta Shakin'*. He relocated to California in the 1960s, and over the years has had his finger in many musical pies. One of the most interesting of these was his production of two albums by screen goddess Mae West, who among other songs recorded both 'N-E-R-V-O-U-S' and 'You Turn Me On'.

SOLO SUPREMACY

On the subject of American success, Adam Faith, one of the UK's top selling singers in the early Sixties, finally cracked the US chart in 1965, which, ironically, was the first year of the decade when he failed to reach the British Top 20. His lone American Top 40 entry came with a Chris Andrews composition, 'It's Alright'. Also debuting in US chart was Faith's best known musical arranger, John Barry, with the self-penned theme to the James Bond film *Goldfinger*, which was the only US singles success for one of the most successful film score composers of the last thirty years. Two more British males who briefly appeared on the Hot 100 were actor/singers Noel Harrison and Davy Jones. Harrison, the son of fellow actor Rex, who was best known for his starring role in the record-breaking musical and film, *My Fair Lady*, enjoyed only limited commercial success, with two folk-flavoured mid-table hits, 'A Young Girl' written by Charles Aznavour, and Leonard Cohen's composition, 'Suzanne'. At the end of the decade, however, he did make the UK Top 10 with 'Windmills Of Your Mind'. In 1965, Davy Jones, who had starred in the musical *Oliver*, managed just a short tenure on the chart with 'What Are We Going To Do?'. That, of course, was far from the last hit Davy Jones stored in his locker, as he returned a year later as one of The Monkees.

After three years of group supremacy, 1966 proved to be very good for solo male singers; with the year's top three British singles coming from Tom Jones, Jim Reeves and Frank Sinatra. Newcomers to the upper reaches of the UK chart that year included folk/rock styled Crispian St. Peters, who had a million seller with 'Pied Piper', Chris Farlowe, whose 'Out Of Time' headed the British chart, and ex-hit group members Alan Price and Paul Jones.

MULTI-TALENTED

Durham-born keyboard player/vocalist Alan Price, had been the original leader of The Animals (see Animals biography), and it was his hypnotic organ led-arrangement of 'House Of The Rising Sun' that helped make it a transatlantic topper. He left the band in 1965 to form The Alan Price Set, and his first single, an update of Chuck Jackson's 'Any Day Now', was a chart casualty. However, the follow-up, a magical revival of Screaming Jay Hawkins' theme song, 'I Put A Spell On You', was his key to the chart, and from 1966 to 1968 Price and his horn-heavy backing band notched up a further four British Top 20 entries; 'Hi Lili Hi Lo', the cute Randy Newman novelty 'Simon Smith & His Amazing Dancing Bear', the self-composed 'The House That Jack Built' and jazzman Sonny Rollins' catchy calypso-styled composition, 'Don't Stop The Carnival'. The multi-talented Price proved to be more than just a recording artist, staying active in the music business long after the Swinging Sixties were history from time to time in collaboration with fellow keyboard player Georgie Fame. The same can also be said of Paul Jones, the voice on Manfred Mann's transatlantic No. 1, 'Do Wah Diddy Diddy'. Jones not only released a handful of

Adam Faith (above) and, at the time of his leading The Alan Price Set, the ex-Animals keyboard man

successful solo singles in his homeland (see Manfred Mann biography) after leaving the group, but also later eased successfully into other areas of the music business.

As a rule, British male vocalists whose chart careers started before 1963 found it impossible to keep the hits flowing throughout the Beat Boom era. Billy Fury, Ken Dodd and Cliff Richard were the main exceptions to that rule. Liverpool's first singer/songwriting hit machine, Billy Fury (real name Ronald Wycherley), was a Presley-esque performer who first hit with the self-composed 'Maybe Tomorrow' in 1959, when he was just 17; and from 1963-66, he doubled his score of UK Top 20 entries to 18. His biggest hits in the second half of his chart career were with Alan Fielding's composition, 'Like I've Never Been Gone', the superior American beat ballad, 'When Will You Say I Love You', and 'In Summer', penned by British vocal trio, The Avons. Ken Dodd was another Liverpool-born artist who had his early chart successes in the days before a Merseyside birthplace was a plus. Dodd is a comedian and family entertainer who occasionally bursts into song during his act. He was an out-and-out MOR singer, who never attempted to rock. Dodd had Top 10 hits in 1966 with 'The River' and 'Promises', but is best known for his million-selling revival of the '30s hit 'Tears', the most successful UK single of 1965.

WELL REGARDED

Cliff Richard has no equals in the annals of British pop music. He has been a consistent hitmaker for 36 years, amassing more Top 20 hits than any other artist including Elvis Presley. In the Beat Boom era, the 'Peter Pan of Pop' added 18 Top 20 singles to the 22 he had previously amassed, and clocked up another eight Top 10 albums. Among the singles were three chart toppers, 'The Next Time', the Shadows-composed theme to his hit film, *Summer Holiday*, and the Nashville-recorded country ballad, 'The Minute You're Gone', which had previously been a Stateside success for Sonny James. One-time skiffle group member and coffee bar singer Richard has broken almost every conceivable British record in his career, which spans five decades, and is now heading towards his unprecedented 100th British Top 20 entry.

It's all showbiz: Ken Dodd with the 'Show Business Personality of the Year' award for 1965 (above), while Cliff attends an event with pantomime co-star Pippa Steele

A few well-regarded British singers scored their biggest single successes in 1966, although the records in question only reached the lower regions of the UK Top 30. One such artist was the London-born one-time actor and ex-member of both The Trends and The Riot Squad, Graham Bonney. This vocalist and ex-session guitarist, who had penned his solo debut disc, 'My Little World Is All Blue', co wrote his second single, 'Supergirl', with Barry Mason. Somehow this extremely catchy composition failed to fly up the British charts. However, in Germany it deservedly shot to the top faster than a speeding bullet, selling over a million copies en route. Neil Christian, who had recorded several unsuccessful singles for Columbia in the early 1960s, also had his only notable slice of chart action in 1966 with the infectious 'That's Nice'. Christian, one of the more talented members of the almost-made-it team, is probably best remembered for the fact that his backing band, The Crusaders, at times included gifted guitarists Jimmy Page and Albert Lee. MOR balladeer Vince Hill was arguably the most frequently heard pop singer on BBC radio in the early 1960s (when live vocalists were featured as often as records). He had his first chart entry with an English interpretation of Edith Piaf's French success, 'La Vie En Rose', entitled 'Take Me To Your Heart Again'. Incidentally, before going solo Hill had been a member of The Raindrops (with hit composer Johnny Worth) and, like Julie Rogers, had sung with Teddy Foster's Orchestra.

The final two male artists to debut in the UK Top 30 in 1966 were the operatically-trained Liverpudlian David Garrick and R&B performer Zoot Money. The nattily dressed and photogenic Garrick's (real name Philip Core) early experience included playing at the Cavern in a group tagged The Dions. His first two solo singles drummed up little interest, but in 1966 he nearly reached the Top 20 with both 'Lady Jane', a cover of the Rolling Stones song, and 'Dear Mrs. Appleby', a novelty number first put on record by the oddly named Flip Cartridge's (real name Billy Meshel). Zoot (born George) Money is another well-known music business character whose chart track record does not equate with his stature in the Swinging Sixties. Ace showman Money formed his first Big Roll Band in the early 1960s and released his first single, an interesting interpretation of The Daylighters dance ditty, 'The Uncle Willie', in 1964. The visually entertaining ensemble, whose music veered towards the less commercial jazz end of the R&B spectrum, had their one brief brush with chart fame, thanks to their mini-hit, 'Big Time Operator', and Money later worked in America with Eric Burdon & The New Animals.

All-in-all, the Beat Boom was both harmful and helpful to the plight of British solo singers. On one hand, groups unceremoniously shoved soloists out of the spotlight, trampling many underfoot, yet on the other, they widened the world market for all British recordings. By the end of the era, solo singers were starting to re-claim some of their share of the UK market, and many were also enjoying the added benefits of big transatlantic sales.

HEINZ

German-born and Southampton-bred vocalist/bass player, Heinz Burt, had two of his bands rejected by Joe Meek, before this top producer decided to take him under his wing. Meek recalled 'There was a chance of fitting him in with The Outlaws, but that fell through, so I decided to build a group around him - that's how convinced I was of his personal magnetism.' That group became Meek's studio backing band, The Tornados. After the world-wide success of their single, 'Telstar', Meek came to the conclusion that the time was right for Heinz to attempt a solo vocal career, even though, to quote

Meek, 'He was sometimes out of tune - a bit flat.' Despite much hype, his first solo Decca single, 'Dreams Do Come True' fell flat. The song incidentally was featured in Heinz' solo film debut, *Farewell Performance* (he later also appeared in the equally obscure pop movie *Live It Up*). His first solo tour, on which The Wild Boys (including a young Ritchie Blackmore - later of Deep Purple) accompanied him, also proved less than successful, as rockers almost continuously heckled him, when he ill-advisedly supported Jerry Lee Lewis and Gene Vincent. Heinz' only major hit came in 1963, with the Joe Meek produced and Geoff Goddard composed tribute to the late US rock'n'roll great, Eddie Cochran, 'Just Like Eddie'. At the time of this hit, Meek proudly stated, 'I've had this feeling of certainty all the way that he's destined for very big things in the world of show business.' In 1964, Heinz announced that he was gunning for Cliff Richard's crown, but the only ammunition he mustered were the minor hits 'Country Boy', 'You Were There' and 'Questions I Can't Answer' and a revival of the old blues-cum-skiffle song, 'Digging My Potatoes' . Heinz, who had everything short of a truly distinctive or outstanding voice, has often been seen since on the cabaret and revival circuits.

DAVE BERRY

In 1961, Sheffield-born Dave Grundy joined The Cruisers (previously known as Chuck Fowler's R&B band). A year later, Mickie Most spotted the group, recorded some demos with them, and brought them to the attention of Decca A&R man Mike Smith. They joined that label in early 1963, following a two-month tenure at Hamburg's famous Top Ten Club. After much deliberation, 'Memphis Tennessee' was chosen as the ideal debut vehicle for this unusual performer, and his version made the UK Top 20 alongside Chuck Berry's original. Dave Berry followed this with minor hit revivals of 'My Baby Left Me' (previously recorded by Arthur Crudup and Elvis Presley) and 'Baby It's You' (a US million seller for The Shirelles, which The Beatles also covered). Berry got annoyed when people harped on about his continually reviving songs, angrily stating 'They don't realise that I'm a bigger fan than they are of these discs.' He later added 'I don't find anything wrong with recording someone else's numbers,' emphasising 'I am not trying to better the first recording.' Although he personally did not initially rate the song highly, 'The Crying Game', penned for him by British tunesmith Geoff Stephens (the megaphoned voice on the New Vaudeville Band's US chart topper 'Winchester Cathedral'), became the first of his three British Top 10 entries. This trio of hits also included covers of Bobby Goldsboro's US biggie, 'Little Things' (which took Berry almost 30 takes to get right), in 1965, and the sentimental 'Mama' in 1966, a song with which balladeer B.J. Thomas had scored Stateside. Berry's much discussed stage act helped make him a top star in Europe. In the Netherlands, for example, his single 'This Strange Effect', was one of the biggest-selling 45s ever. It also got him tagged 'immoral, sick and a bad influence' by German judges in the 1965 European Singing Cup (where he walked away with the Press Prize as top act). Berry, arguably the first pop star to show a real interest in Eastern religions, greatly influenced the stage act of 1970's UK superstar Alvin Stardust, and was also revered by several stars of the later UK punk scene. Despite being seen on several US TV shows (filmed in the UK), American success eluded the colourful character until 1993, when his original version of the 'The Crying Game' appeared on the hit soundtrack album of a similarly titled film.

GEORGIE FAME

When he was only 16, Manchester-born singer/keyboard player Georgie Fame (real name Clive Powell) went on tour with Americans Eddie Cochran and Gene Vincent, and a year later in 1961, he compered a Larry Parnes package show and

At the eleventh hour, Eric Burdon's first solo release was switched from 'Mama Told Me Not To Come' to ' Help Me Girl'

Dave Berry, he of the hand-held stage act all of his own

joined Billy Fury's backing band, The Blue Flames. When Fury replaced the group with The Tornados in 1962, Fame & The Blue Flames took up a residency at London's famous Flamingo Club, where their mixture of jazz-influenced R&B and Blue Beat (an early version of reggae) was very well received by a predominately black audience. He released several records on Columbia, including the ground-breaking live LP, Rhythm & Blues At The Flamingo, before his version of 'Yeh Yeh' (a minor US hit in 1963 for Mongo Santamaria) topped the UK chart in 1965 and reached US Top 20 in *Cash Box*. The follow-up, 'In The Meantime', composed by fellow British jazz pianist Johnny Burch, returned him to the British Top 20, and in 1966 he had notable UK hits with his distinctive treatments of Bobby Hebb's hook-filled 'Sunny', Billy Stewart's American R&B success, 'Sitting In The Park', and his own gimmicky but worthy composition 'Get Away', which climbed into the British Top 3. After disbanding The Blue Flames, Fame scored with the self-penned 'Because I Love You', and in 1967 returned to the top spot in Britain with the commercial Mitch Murray & Peter Callander composition, 'The Ballad Of Bonnie & Clyde'. For the record, the latter song, which was suggested by the celebrated gangster movie, gave this distinctive vocalist his only US Top 10 single. Subsequently, Fame moved closer to cabaret, particularly when he formed a duo with ex-Animals keyboard star Alan Price, which resulted in a British Top 10 hit in 1971 with 'Rosetta'. Georgie Fame proved that the pop buying public could enjoy an injection of jazzy R&B in their music, and remains a respected figure. In 1989, he worked as Van Morrison's keyboard player and musical director, while continuing as an active (if not overly successful) solo recording artist.

TOM JONES

Thomas Woodward, who hailed from South Wales, started singing as Tommy Scott (backed by both The Senators and The Playboys), and for a while was even known as Tiger Tom before being re-named Tom Jones after the hero of the then popular film. After an unsuccessful period with producer Joe Meek, Jones joined Decca and his first chart single, 'It's Not Unusual', zipped to No. 1 in Britain and into the American Top 10. Incidentally, this record, which featured Jimmy Page's guitar work, also returned to the UK Top 20 in 1987. To date, Jones has had 11 American Top 20 singles and was still adding to his impressive tally of British Top 20 singles in 1993. On the singles front, he is probably best known for his cut of 'Green Green Grass of Home' (first recorded by country singer Johnny Darrell), which sold over a million in the UK alone. His other major transatlantic hits include: the film theme, 'What's New Pussycat', in 1965, 'I'll Never Fall In Love Again' (a standout ballad written and earlier recorded by Britain's skiffle supremo Lonnie Donegan) in 1967, and the karaoke classic, 'Delilah', the following year. Jones, who had more adult appeal than the majority of his UK pop music peers, hosted his own transatlantic TV series, *The Tom Jones Show*, in the late 1960s. He was also no slouch when it came to selling albums, amassing 10 gold LPs in the US and a dozen British Top 10 entries. Additionally, he is no stranger to the American R&B, Dance Music, Easy Listening and Country charts, with no less than 16 of his singles entering the latter - a record for a British act. This soulful MOR-slanted singer, with a timeless sex appeal, has been rightly regarded as one of the world's top entertainers.

DONOVAN

A Scottish-born folk singer/songwriter, Donovan Leitch was regarded as the UK's version of Bob Dylan - they both played guitar, wore caps and blew raucously into harmonicas - although Donovan actually based himself on American wandering minstrel Woody Guthrie, who also influenced Dylan. After big hits in 1965 with

In 1964, Paul Raven (Gary Glitter) and Gerry Dorsey (Englebert Humperdinck) were still struggling without success

Tom Jones in action, another star who graced the MOR mecca of the 1960's, London's Talk Of The Town night spot

the wistful 'Catch The Wind' and 'Colours', which both made the UK Top 10 and were also hits in America, Donovan became a client of hotshot producer Mickie Most, who supervised his Pye recordings for the next three years, during which time all of his biggest hits were released. His most successful British single, 'Sunshine Superman', which topped the American chart, presented a folk/rock singer with a harder edge than the more gentle, earlier model, and this was followed by another gold record, 'Mellow Yellow', which was arranged by John Paul Jones (later of Led Zeppelin) featuring a whispered backing vocal track by Paul McCartney. Further hits were periodically released, including 'There Is A Mountain' in 1967, 'Hurdy Gurdy Man', a transatlantic Top 10 single the following year, and 1969's 'Goo Goo Barabajagal', on which he shared the label credit with another of Most's artists, guitarist Jeff Beck. Donovan, who wrote virtually all his own material, was an essential part of Swinging London, performing with The Beatles on their history-making satellite TV appearance which produced 'All You Need Is Love', and becoming a disciple of the celebrated Maharishi Mahesh Yogi. By 1970, his fame had faded and the hits had all but disappeared. However, he remains a respected performer and is now recording again, albeit enjoying cult status rather than mainstream appeal, and a 1990 album 'Rising' appeared after several mentions of his influence by contemporary bands including Happy Mondays.

The apparent fued between Bob Dylan and Donovan (left) was fuelled by their on-screen encounter in the Dylan tour documentary *Don't Look Back*

JONATHAN KING

Londoner Jonathan (real Christian name Kenneth) King was an ex-pupil of the famous Charterhouse public school. After failing to interest producer Joe Meek in his talents, noted music entrepreneur and one time host of TV's *Oh Boy!* Tony Hall helped him to land a deal with Decca Records. King's debut outing, 'Everyone's Gone To The Moon', was a substantial transatlantic seller. Lack of further vocal success in the 1960s did not deter King; he simply side-stepped into TV, music journalism and production, and his uncanny knack for spotting British hits earned him a senior executive post with Decca. In the 1970s, King, who had self-confidence to spare, virtually took up residence in the UK singles chart. During that decade, he not only had British hits under his own name, but also scaled the best sellers with an assortment of one-off hits under guises such as The Weathermen, Father Abraphart & The Smurps, Bubblerock, 53rd & 3rd, Sound 9418, 100 Ton

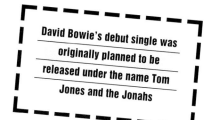

David Bowie's debut single was originally planned to be released under the name Tom Jones and the Jonahs

& A Feather, Sakkarin and Shag. To add to this covetable collection, the erstwhile pop svengali produced unpretentious pop hits for The Piglets and St. Cecilia, and helped launch the careers of both The Bay City Rollers and 10cc. In addition to this, King, whose critics accused him of aiming his records at the so-called lowest common denominator, also ran his own successful label, UK Records. The outspoken yet likeable King is still confident that, if given a free hand, he could resolve many problems facing today's UK music business – and several people in the know believe he might just do that.

CRISPIAN ST. PETERS

Crispian St. Peters (born Robin Peter Smith) was a singer/songwriter/guitarist from Kent. This ex-boxer and pub singer played in the group Beat Formula Three, before recording his first solo single for Decca, 'At This Moment', in early 1965. He first tasted success in 1966 when his revival of We Five's folky 1965 American Top 5 smash, 'You Were On My Mind', climbed into the British Top 3. St. Peters, who on stage was backed by The Puppets, is probably best remembered for his seemingly deluded assertion that that he was a better singer than Elvis Presley, more exciting than Tom Jones and sexier than Dave Berry. He also said, somewhat portentiously, that his stage name 'was a gift from the unknown', and allegedly claimed his compositions compared more than favourably with the classic songs of The Beatles. St. Peters' short career reached its peak when his cover of The Changin' Times' minor 1965 American hit, 'Pied Piper', climbed into both the UK and US Top 5 in 1966. Fame on the scale that St. Peters envisaged was simply never to be.

CHRIS FARLOWE

Chris Farlowe (real name John Henry Deighton) was one of Britain's earliest and most acceptable exponents of R&B. He started his musical career fronting The John Henry skiffle group, who, despite winning the 1957 All English Skiffle Championship, went nowhere fast. Backed by The Thunderbirds (including celebrated guitarist Albert Lee), the gruff-voiced Farlowe released his first record, an explosive cover of Ray & Bob's small US R&B hit, 'Air Travel', in 1962. He joined Columbia the following year, but his handful of singles (most of which were cover versions) on

Bill Oddie, later a star of
BBC Television's *The Goodies*,
had an unsuccessful single
release in 1964

that label also failed to persuade the public to part with their pennies. After four years of critical acclaim and moderate sales, Farlowe's long overdue chart debut came when his distinctive version of Jagger & Richard's song, 'Think', crept into the Top 20 in 1966. The follow-up, 'Out Of Time', also taken from the Rolling Stones' self-penned album, Aftermath, then took the craggy-voiced Londoner to the top, and gave Immediate Records their first British No. 1. The future looked bright for Farlowe, who was voted Best New Singer of 1966 by *RM* readers. However, his US label, MGM, was unable to create any interest Stateside for 'Out Of Time', and his British success proved to be short-term, future single releases being far less fruitful. Numerous come-backs, though warmly received, have failed to return him to the singles charts, although in 1988, he was a guest vocalist, with Robert Plant, on Jimmy Page's transatlantic Top 30 album, Outrider.

**Chris Farlowe's limited popular
success never matched his
well-deserved reputation among
both musicians and critics**

Dynamic duos

THE DOUBLE ACTS

**The Caravelles, the only all-female
act in the pop top twosomes**

Rock'n'roll was a couple of years old before it finally found its first really major duo, The Everly Brothers, who like all the most successful duos of the early rock era were from the USA. In the early 1960s, America still had more than its share of duos. The best selling ones were the teenage sweethearts Paul & Paula, husband and wife team Steve Lawrence & Eydie Gorme, and siblings Nino Tempo & April Stevens, all of whom scored transatlantic hits. Among the other successful recording couples of that time were Dale & Grace, Dick & Dee Dee, Don & Juan, The Fendermen, and wild twosomes Ike & Tina Turner and Don Gardner & Dee Dee Ford, who also had major American hits before the onset of the Beat Boom.

In the pre-Beatles period, apart from hit novelty couplings such as Peter Sellers & Sophia Loren and Mike Sarne & Wendy Richard (or Billie Davis), the best twosomes Britain had on offer were the dated duo Pearl Carr & Teddy Johnson, country and western couple Miki & Griff and the Everly Brothers wanna-bes The Allisons and The Brook Bros. In truth, this was not the kind of pop potential to whet the world's appetite, and it was therefore not surprising that no post-war UK duo made more than a minor impression on the US chart until the little-heralded Caravelles became not only the first British duo in the post-war years to scale the heights of the American hit parade, but also the harbingers of the British Invasion.

The Caravelles comprised two Barnet-based teenage singers, Lois Wilkinson and Andrea Simpson. They enjoyed a one-off transatlantic hit with their debut disc, a cute and breathy update of Tennessee Ernie Ford's 'You Don't Have To Be A Baby To Cry'. The press handouts described their style as 'so many Peggy Lees all singing at once,' although a better reference point might be the 1950s American schoolgirl twosome, Patience & Prudence. The Caravelles, who had jazz and folk music backgrounds, first met while working together for a North London garage company. Harry Robinson (of Lord Rockingham's X1) produced them for a company he owned with Chris Blackwell (later founder and supremo of Island Records) and the young women's manager, Chris Peers. The Caravelles worked out their own unique arrangement of 'You Don't Have To Be A Baby To Cry', a song which Tony Pitt (guitarist with Alex Welsh's trad jazz band) had suggested they record. This first release took them into the UK Top 10 and the American Top 3, which resulted in their securing a slot on the Beatles' first ever US live show in Washington. The Caravelles, named after a French airplane, released several similar sounding singles but none of the others took off.

Carter-Lewis were the first British male duo to find themselves in the UK Top 20 after the birth of the Beat Boom. They were singer/songwriters John Carter (real name John Shakespeare) and Ken Lewis (real name James Hawker). The duo, together with their backing band, The Southerners, were often heard on the top UK pop radio shows of the early 1960s. Despite this exposure, their records on Piccadilly and Ember were consigned to oblivion. Their sole chart success came with their second Oriole outing, 'Your Momma's Out Of Town', which briefly slipped into the UK Top 20 in late 1963. As songwriters, Carter & Lewis hit in 1962 with the cockney novelty, 'Will I What', performed by another British duo, Mike Sarne & Billie Davis. In 1963 they penned one of the most under-rated records of the Beat Boom, the stomping 'That's What I Want' by The Marauders, and a year later Brenda Lee had a transatlantic Top 20 entry with these skilled pop craftsmen's bouncy composition, 'Is It True'. Both Carter and Lewis composed many more hits in the 1960s, and had several successful singles in their own right as members of The Ivy League , First Class and The Flowerpot Men.

Duo becomes trio, as Carter-Lewis become The Ivy League

1963 saw the launch of the first (short-lived) visual jukebox in Great Britain, which was known as the Scopitone

DEBUT OF THE DUOS

There is a strong possibility that - excluding Batman & Robin - the best known male twosome in the mid-1960s was Peter & Gordon. Messrs. Asher & Waller, the first British duo to make a sustained impression on both sides of the Atlantic, amassed eight American and five UK Top 20 singles between 1964-1966. This gentle duo's enviable portfolio of pop hits was characterised by the fact that many of their best known singles were either composed by Lennon & McCartney or were revivals. The two Beatles penned Peter & Gordon's first release, a tuneful transatlantic chart-topper titled 'A World Without Love', as well as their big hits, 'Nobody I Know', 'I Don't Want To See You Again' and 'Woman'. When they were accused of relying too much on Beatles material, Waller retorted, 'Elvis and the Everly Brothers used the same songwriters for God-knows-how-many-years and nobody had a go at them'. Asher defended their revival records by saying,

'Some revivals and covers are so similar they're just diabolical – however, if you give an old song your own interpretation, what's wrong with that?' The duo, who insisted their Beatle haircuts pre-dated the Mop Tops, did not claim to be the most exciting live band in the Beat Boom. Asher himself confessed 'I always have the uncontrollable urge to yawn in the middle of a song' – nevertheless, in the mid-1960s the twosome played to packed houses (even when other British acts were performing to less than capacity US crowds) on both continents and built a formidable fan following.

Just two weeks after Peter & Gordon debuted on the US chart with 'A World Without Love', another British duo, Chad Stuart & Jeremy Clyde, joined them. It was to be the first of nearly a dozen visits to the American Top 100 for them. Despite their laudable American success, Chad & Jeremy remained an almost unknown quantity in their homeland, never even managing a minor hit. The duo spent much of the mid 1960s on tour in the USA where they were, as often as not, greeted by hundreds of hysterical, screaming teenage girls. Nonetheless, they disliked package shows, describing them as being 'a miserable waste of time for both artists and audience' adding, 'unless young people are presented with something new in entertainment, rock'n'roll and personal appearances will die a grim death.' The earliest advertisements for the duo in the USA described their music as 'The Oxford Sound', adding that it was 'as English as a cup of tea' and claimed Jeremy was the grandson of the Duke Of Wellington (which would have made him very much older).

"I always have the uncontrollable urge to yawn in the middle of a song"

Peter Asher

Photographer Gered Mankovitz said this picture of Paul and Barry Ryan was inspired by David Bailey's *Box Of Pin-Ups* collection

However their records were by no means every Englishman's cup of tea, and Chad & Jeremy only earned their 'Upper-Class-Heroes' status Stateside. Unlike either Peter & Gordon or Chad & Jeremy, Paul & Barry Ryan (real name Sapherson) had no folk music leanings; they were an out-and-out pop duo and as such had no equal in Britain in the 1960s. The twin sons of 1950s singing star Marion Ryan and impresario Harold Davidson started in show business when aged 15. Their first four releases hit the UK Top 30, with the potent pop ditties, 'Don't Bring Me Your Heartaches' and 'I Love Her', making the biggest impression. Even though the photogenic pair were featured in several US teenybop magazines, and appeared on *Hullaballoo*, their American sales were negligible. By 1968, the pressures of show business resulted in Paul Ryan having a nervous breakdown, which brought an end to the siblings' duo days. Barry said of the incident, 'There's something wrong with the pop world when a boy of 19 gets into the state Paul was in.' He emphasised 'it was the politics of the business that got him down.' In late 1968, Barry's second solo single, the show-stopping stomper 'Eloise', topped the UK and German charts and cracked the US Top 100. The song, which Paul penned, went on to sell over three million copies world-wide for Barry and returned to the UK Top 3 in 1986 by The Damned. Paul, who also wrote Frank Sinatra's 1971 UK Top 20 entry, 'I Will Drink The Wine', died of cancer in 1992 aged 44.

BACK SEAT

The last British duo to write their names in the transatlantic chart book in the Beat Boom years were David & Jonathan, who, like Carter-Lewis, were songwriters using a stage name for recording. The duo were Bristol based Roger (David) Greenaway and Roger (Jonathan) Cook, who started singing together in the underrated doo-wopping pop group, The Kestrels. In 1965, the pair tasted both success and failure; their composition, 'You've Got Your Troubles', sold a million by The Fortunes, but the duo's debut disc as David & Jonathan, 'Laughing Fit To Cry', was universally ignored. Producer George Martin suggested that for their second single they record 'Michelle', a track he had cut with The Beatles for their Rubber Soul album. It was an inspired idea, and their interpretation of the tender ballad not only made the UK Top 10 (The Overlanders' recording reached No. 1), but also reached the American Top 20, out-pointing all the other versions.

The two Rogers: top songwriters Greenaway and Cook in their previous role as David and Jonathan

A couple of months later David & Jonathan had their biggest British hit, the bouncy 'Lovers Of The World Unite'. In the States, this song, which they had written on the coach between shows on a Herman's Hermits tour, was covered by successful American group, The Vogues, but neither version charted. Further releases by the duo ran aground and even their version of The Beatles' album track, 'She's Leaving Home', failed to stop them sinking. As demand for David & Jonathan records decreased, demand for Greenaway and Cook compositions grew, and the multi-talented twosome went on to become one of the most successful songwriting teams in the history of British pop music.

At the same time that David & Jonathan were escorting 'Michelle' into the Top 20, The Truth's recording of 'Girl', another Beatles' song from their Rubber Soul album, gave the London-based duo their sole flirtation with fame. The Truth were ex-hairdressers, Steven Gold and Francis Aiello, and their name was supposedly inspired by the Ray Charles song, 'Tell The Truth'. 'Girl', which was their third single, was engaged in a chart skirmish with the St. Louis Union version of the same song. The Truth's treatment fared marginally better than that of the Manchester group. Gold attributed their victory partly to Johnny Harris' arrangement and partly to the fact St. Louis Union had 'crippled a lovely song.' When asked his thoughts about other duos, Gold (who, under the name Nosmo King, had a minor UK hit in 1974 with 'Goodbye Nothing To Say') replied, 'Peter & Gordon are very confident and experienced, but don't have much personality, and in my opinion, no other duo comes close to The Righteous Brothers.'

Gold was almost certainly not alone in the opinion that, even at the height of the British Beat boom, UK duos still took a back seat to their American cousins. There was no arguing with the fact that acts like Peter & Gordon and Chad & Jeremy sold vast quantities of records in the mid-1960s, but if people were asked to list the most important, innovative, interesting or exciting duos of the era, then surely most would place American acts like The Righteous Brothers, Sonny & Cher, Simon & Garfunkel or Sam & Dave above them.

PETER & GORDON

Londoner Peter Asher made his film debut as an eight year old in a 1952 Jack Hawkins movie, *The Planter's Wife* (US title *Outpost In Malaya*), and was also seen in seven episodes of the popular mid-1950s TV series, *Robin Hood*. He befriended Scottish-born Gordon Waller whilst both were studying at the Westminster Boys Public School, and they started singing together in coffee bars in the early 1960s. Norman Newell signed them to Columbia on the recommendation of a friend, who had seen them at London's trendy Pickwick Club. Asher's sister Jane persuaded her then boyfriend, Paul McCartney, to complete a song he had part-finished for the duo, 'A World Without Love'. That song became not only the wholesome

Kevin Godley and Graham Gouldman, later of 10cc, debuted with The Mockingbirds' 'That's How' on Columbia

Gordon Waller (on the right) of Peter and Gordon, later did an Elvis impersonation in the musical *Joseph And The Amazing Technicolor Dreamcoat*

"I don't suppose a couple like us can stay on top all that long – I think it will just be a couple of years"
Peter Asher

upper middle-class duo's first release, but also the biggest of their many hits, easily outselling an American cover version by ex-teen idol Bobby Rydell. Other significant singles by the soft rockers included: 'True Love Ways' (a Buddy Holly ballad), 'To Know You Is To Love You' (written by Phil Spector), 'Baby I'm Yours' (first recorded by US R&B star Barbara Lewis), 'I Go To Pieces' (a Del Shannon song) plus the near-novelties 'Lady Godiva' and 'Knight In Rusty Armour' (both composed by Mike Leander - who later co-wrote Gary Glitter's hits). Early in their career, Asher prophesied, 'I don't suppose a couple like us can stay on top all that long - I think it will just be a couple of years.' In reality the duo finally called it a day in early 1968. Waller released several solo singles without success, while Asher went on to become one of the most successful producers (for the record, his first attempt had been producing The Aztecs for EMI in 1964) of the rock era. He was the person at the controls for a string of platinum albums during the Seventies by both James Taylor and Linda Ronstadt, and twice won the Grammy for Best Producer Of The Year.

CHAD & JEREMY

Chad Stuart and Jeremy Clyde had similar backgrounds to Peter & Gordon, since all of them were ex-public school boys who had an interest in folk-orientated music. Chad & Jeremy first met when they were studying at London's Central School of Speech and Drama, and before long the two singer/guitarists were performing together. In late 1963, they signed to the comparatively small English label, Ember, who placed them with a fellow independent label, World Artists, in America. The act struggled to gain recognition in Britain but US success was swift. Their debut disc, the melodic 'Yesterday's Gone', narrowly missed the US Top 20. This inspired the twosome to pack their bags and go west to California (unlike many later British acts, they appeared to have had no real permit problems). Before the end of '66, Chad & Jeremy had put another six soft sounding folk/rock singles into the American Top 40, and had seen half a dozen of their albums climb into the US Top 100. Their biggest singles were 'A Summer Song' (which, like their debut record, was co-written by Stuart and released under their full names), the oldie 'Willow Weep For Me', and Van McCoy's composition, 'Before And After'. The last of these was on Columbia, the label the duo joined in mid-1965. During their hit spell, apart from appearing on the usual US pop TV shows, they also had acting roles in top rated family TV programmes such as *Dick Van Dyke Show* and *Batman* (in which Cat Woman pur(r)loined their voices). In 1967, they released one of the earliest concept albums, Of Cabbages And Kings, but after its relative failure they decided to go their separate ways. Since then both Chad & Jeremy have had some success in the acting arena, and Clyde has also made a minor mark producing and arranging. In the early Eighties they briefly re-united to record an eponymous album for Rockshire. They still had the sound which made them successful in the 1960s, but to quote their first hit 'that was yesterday and yesterday's gone'.

The picture from the Chad and Jeremy session below that wasn't used anywhere had the duo with their backs to the camera using a (very) public urinal!

Andrew Oldham discoveries, the duo Twice As Much, released their version of Jagger and Richards' 'Sittin' On A Fence'

Byrds, Monkees and Turtles

Groups and duos had always been a pivotal part of American pop music. In fact, in the year before the first wave of British invaders, only eight of the Top 20 US singles acts were solo artists; if there was one thing on which the success of the attack could not be blamed, it was the shortage of US groups.

When The Beatles and the rest of the rockin' redcoats arrived, it was America's teen-targeted artists who were most affected, as the look and sound of their British contemporaries made many of them appear old-fashioned overnight.

The US groups faring best in 1964 were those in the R&B and surf music areas. R&B, in its original American form, positively thrived throughout the Beat Boom, with Motown groups like The Four Tops, The Temptations and The Supremes scoring their first big hits in 1964, alongside their UK cousins. Surf too rode out the initial overseas offensive well, with 1964 debut hits coming to Californian groups The Rip Chords, The Marketts and bald instrumental band The Pyramids. Also helping to put L.A. and Liverpool, and Malibu and Merseyside, side by side in the American charts, were West Coast combos The Premiers (whose hit, 'Farmer John', was originally recorded by R&B duo Don & Dewey), The Hondells and female trio The Murmaids. Minneapolis punk-surfers The Trashmen collected a gold record for their excruciating but excellent 'Surfin' Bird' (based on R&B group The Rivington's 'Papa-Oom-Mow-Mow') and Ronny & The Daytonas proved surf hits could come from Nashville cats. Indiana's Rivieras also

The Supremes at London Airport, October 1964 (left to right) Florence Ballard, Diana Ross and Mary Wilson. Opposite, the Byrds with (back row) Gene Clark, Roger McGuinn, Mike Clark (front) Chris Hillman, David Crosby

1964-66
TOP SINGLES ARTISTS IN THE US

1	**THE BEATLES** CAPITOL *UK*
2	**THE SUPREMES** MOTOWN *US*
3	**THE BEACH BOYS** CAPITOL *US*
4	**HERMAN'S HERMITS** MGM *UK*
5	**THE ROLLING STONES** LONDON *UK*
6	**THE DAVE CLARK FIVE** EPIC *UK*
7	**THE FOUR SEASONS** PHILIPS *US*
8	**GARY LEWIS & THE PLAYBOYS** LIBERTY *US*
9	**THE RIGHTEOUS BROTHERS** PHILLES *US*
10	**JOHNNY RIVERS** IMPERIAL *US*
11	**LOVIN' SPOONFUL** KAMA SUTRA *US*
12	**THE FOUR TOPS** MOTOWN *US*
13	**PETULA CLARK** WARNER *UK*
14	**THE TEMPTATIONS** GORDY *US*
15	**BOBBY VINTON** EPIC *US*
16	**PETER & GORDON** CAPITOL *UK*
17	**ELVIS PRESLEY** RCA *US*
18	**ROGER MILLER** SMASH *US*
19	**SIMON & GARFUNKEL** COLUMBIA *US*
20	**ERIC BURDON & THE ANIMALS** MGM *UK*

briefly rode the crest of a wave with their infectious interpretation of R&B singer Joe Jones' 'California Sun', and even though New York newcomer's The Shangri-Las were hardly surfer girls, they did remember walkin' in the sand.

1965 was a year of changes. American pop groups responded to the Anglo incursion. R&B, which continued to rack up most impressive sales, officially changed its name to soul music, and folk crashed head-on into rock, producing a style that would return America to the forefront of popular music.

THE LIMEY INFLUENCE

The magnitude of the 1964 assault may have knocked the USA sidewards, but American groups quickly got their acts together. They absorbed the sound, songs, feel and image of their British counterparts, and by early 1965 a new breed of longer-haired, hipper looking American bands were ready to reclaim the allegiance of US teenagers. Among the first of these to hit in their homeland were West Coast outfits Gary Lewis & The Playboys and The Beau Brummels (produced by Sly Stone - later leader of Sly & The Family Stone). They were soon followed by a Tex-Mex band with an English name, The Sir Douglas Quintet, and tinsel-town trio Dino, Desi & Billy, who, like Gary Lewis, were the sons of Hollywood celebrities. Before the year was out, many more Brit-influenced pop bands broke through, including The Castaways from Minnesota, Memphis group The Gentrys (who revived 'Keep On Dancing' by The Aventis), The Dallas-based Five Americans, Chicago combo The New Colony Six and New Jersey natives The Knickerbockers, who took Beatle-cloning to new heights. There were also many more obvious cash-in combos like The British Walkers, Liverpool Five and The American Beatles, who, perhaps not surprisingly, failed to find favour with the American public. The majority of these new groups found fame not only fleeting, but also unable to travel across the Atlantic. Of the new pop outfits, only The McCoys (with the memorable 'Hang On Sloopy' initially recorded by soul group

	TITLE	ARTIST
1	I WANT TO HOLD YOUR HAND	THE BEATLES
2	I'M A BELIEVER	THE MONKEES
3	(I CAN'T GET NO) SATISFACTION	THE ROLLING STONES
4	THERE I'VE SAID IT AGAIN	BOBBY VINTON
5	BABY LOVE	THE SUPREMES
6	CAN'T BUY ME LOVE	THE BEATLES
7	WINCHESTER CATHEDRAL	THE NEW VAUDEVILLE BAND
8	HELLO, DOLLY!	LOUIS ARMSTRONG
9	SHE LOVES YOU	THE BEATLES
10	OH PRETTY WOMAN	ROY ORBISON
11	YESTERDAY	THE BEATLES
12	(YOU'RE MY) SOUL & INSPIRATION	THE RIGHTEOUS BROTHERS
13	TURN! TURN! TURN!	THE BYRDS
14	MRS BROWN YOU'VE GOT A LOVELY DAUGHTER	HERMAN'S HERMITS
15	YOU'VE LOST THAT LOVIN' FEELIN'	THE RIGHTEOUS BROTHERS
16	I CAN'T HELP MYSELF	THE FOUR TOPS
17	WE CAN WORK IT OUT	THE BEATLES
18	GOOD VIBRATIONS	THE BEACH BOYS
19	HOUSE OF THE RISING SUN	THE ANIMALS
20	COME SEE ABOUT ME	THE SUPREMES

Opposite, Mr and Mrs Salvatore Bono, better known to the world at large as Sonny and Cher

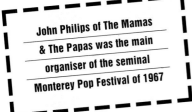

John Philips of The Mamas & The Papas was the main organiser of the seminal Monterey Pop Festival of 1967

The Vibrations) and L.A. trio The Walker Brothers (who had to relocate to Britain to find fame) were warmly welcomed in the UK with chart successes to match.

In the spring of 1965, The Byrds released their version of 'Mr. Tambourine Man', a song taken from Bob Dylan's epic electric album, Bringing It All Back Home. These two records put folk/rock on the map, which helped acts like Sonny & Cher (who grossed $3 million that year), The Turtles and The Lovin' Spoonful to find their way to fame later that year. Britain too fell for folk/rock, and the listing of the UK's top selling artists of 1965 included The Byrds and Sonny & Cher alongside fellow American groups, The Righteous Brothers, Sam The Sham and The Everly Brothers.

CALIFORNIA DREAMIN'

California was the trend-setting state in the Beat Boom era, with San Francisco being hotly tipped as the world's next major musical centre. It was there in late 1965 that Jefferson Airplane made their debut, The Warlocks re-named themselves The Grateful Dead and acid rock was born. By early 1966, L.A. based hippy harmony quartet, The Mamas & The Papas, were saturating the airwaves, and there was a massive migration of musicians to San Francisco's Haight Street. In L.A.,

1964-66
TOP GROUPS/DUOS IN THE US

1	**THE BEATLES**	CAPITOL *UK*
2	**THE SUPREMES**	MOTOWN *US*
3	**THE BEACH BOYS**	CAPITOL *US*
4	**HERMAN'S HERMITS**	MGM *UK*
5	**THE ROLLING STONES**	LONDON *UK*
6	**THE DAVE CLARK FIVE**	EPIC *UK*
7	**THE FOUR SEASONS**	PHILIPS *US*
8	**GARY LEWIS & THE PLAYBOYS**	LIBERTY *US*
9	**THE RIGHTEOUS BROTHERS**	PHILLES *US*
10	**THE LOVIN' SPOONFUL**	KAMA SUTRA *US*
11	**THE FOUR TOPS**	MOTOWN *US*
12	**THE TEMPTATIONS**	GORDY *US*
13	**PETER & GORDON**	CAPITOL *UK*
14	**SIMON & GARFUNKEL**	COLUMBIA *US*
15	**ERIC BURDON & THE ANIMALS**	MGM *UK*
16	**THE KINKS**	REPRISE *UK*
17	**THE SHANGRI-LAS**	RED BIRD *US*
18	**THE MAMAS & THE PAPAS**	DUNHILL *US*
19	**THE BYRDS**	COLUMBIA *US*
20	**THE MONKEES**	COLGEMS *US*

The Beach Boys recorded their revolutionary Pet Sounds album, Buffalo Springfield formed, and The Mothers Of Invention cut their Freak Out album. Also that year, revolutionary L.A. bands Love and The Seeds made their chart debuts, and a big buzz built around San Francisco outfits Quicksilver Messenger Service, Moby Grape, Big Brother & The Holding Company (and their new vocalist Janis Joplin) and Country Joe & The Fish. West Coast groups were not only experimenting with music but also with their names, many of them dropping 'The' as they conjured up hippy handles to suit their style of music. For the first time in the history of rock, record companies were actively seeking out artists with album, rather than singles, sales potential, and California was where many such combos congregated.

EAST COASTIN'

1966 was not only another good year for American R&B groups it was also an amazingly fruitful one for new American rock and beat bands. Long hit runs were started by Paul Revere (named after an American hero in the first battles with the British) & The Raiders, Mitch Ryder & The Detroit Wheels, the highly touted New York quartet The Young Rascals and Tommy James & The Shondells

1964-66
TOP MALE ARTISTS IN THE US

1. **JOHNNY RIVERS**
   IMPERIAL *US*

2. **BOBBY VINTON**
   EPIC *US*

3. **ELVIS PRESLEY**
   RCA *US*

4. **ROGER MILLER**
   SMASH *US*

5. **BOB DYLAN**
   COLUMBIA *US*

6. **MARVIN GAYE**
   TAMLA *US*

7. **DEAN MARTIN**
   REPRISE *US*

8. **JAMES BROWN**
   KING *US*

9. **ROY ORBISON**
   MONUMENT *US*

10. **DONOVAN**
    EPIC *UK*

11. **STEVIE WONDER**
    TAMLA *US*

12. **FRANK SINATRA**
    REPRISE *US*

13. **PERCY SLEDGE**
    ATLANTIC *US*

14. **RONNIE DOVE**
    DIAMOND *US*

15. **SAM COOKE**
    RCA *US*

16. **GENE PITNEY**
    MUSICOR *US*

17. **LOU CHRISTIE**
    MGM *US*

18. **TOM JONES**
    PARROT *UK*

19. **TOMMY ROE**
    ABC *US*

20. **SSGT. BARRY SADLER**
    RCA *US*

(whose chart topping debut hit, 'Hanky Panky', had originally been released in 1963). Other groups who made their chart debuts included The Bobby Fuller Four (with a revival of The Crickets' catchy 'I Fought The Law'), Carolina octet The Swingin' Medallions fronted by John McElrath and New Jersey combo The Critters, whose Don Ciccone later joined the Four Seasons. Also scoring their initial hit that year were Cleveland quintet The Outsiders (whose chart entries included a rocky revival of 'Respectable' recorded previously by its composers The Isley Brothers), The Royal Guardsmen, who had a run of high flying hits inspired by the cartoon character 'Snoopy', and the New York-based classical-pop quintet, The Left Banke. Garage bands too made good, with so-called punks like The Shadows Of Knight (who hit with Them's calling card 'Gloria'), The Standells (with the classic 'Dirty Water'), ? (Question Mark) & The Mysterians, The Syndicate Of Sound from San Jose and the vampire-ish psychedelic Count Five all managing to crack the US Top 20, and all failing to chart in the UK. Folk/rock also flourished, and from the genre came new groups Simon & Garfunkel (who started the year with a No.1 single), The Association who topped the US chart with the timeless tunes 'Cherish' and 'Windy', and The Cyrkle from Pennsylvania, managed by British Beat Boom baron Brian Epstein.

Among the handful of American groups who made any real impression on the UK chart in 1966 were that year's most adventurous recording act, The Beach Boys. The Californian combo were not only that year's overall Top Singles Artists in Britain, they also replaced The Beatles as World's Top Group in the *NME* poll,

1964-66
TOP FEMALE ARTISTS IN THE US

1	**PETULA CLARK** WARNER *UK*
2	**NANCY SINATRA** REPRISE *US*
3	**DUSTY SPRINGFIELD** PHILIPS *UK*
4	**SHIRLEY ELLIS** CONGRESS *US*
5	**LESLEY GORE** MERCURY *US*
6	**DIONNE WARWICK** SCEPTER *US*
7	**MARY WELLS** MOTOWN *US*
8	**BRENDA LEE** DECCA *US*
9	**BETTY EVERETT** VEE JAY *US*
10	**CHER** IMPERIAL *US*
11	**GALE GARNETT** RCA *US*
12	**MILLIE SMALL** SMASH *WEST INDIES*
13	**FONTELLA BASS** CHECKER *US*
14	**BARBARA MASON** ARTIC *US*
15	**BARBRA STREISAND** COLUMBIA *US*
16	**BARBARA LEWIS** ATLANTIC *US*
17	**ASTRUD GILBERTO** VERVE *US*
18	**DIANE RENAY** 20TH CENTURY *US*
19	**PATTY DUKE** UA *US*
20	**SHIRLEY BASSEY** UA *UK*

and were afforded the kind of reception at London Airport usually reserved for Liverpool's Fab Four. For the record, the only US groups to make their British Top 20 debuts in 1966 were The Mamas & The Papas, The Lovin' Spoonful, The Supremes, The Sandpipers (an L.A. trio who hit with the MOR 'Guantanamera'), The Four Tops and duos Ike & Tina Turner and Simon & Garfunkel.

MADE TO MEASURE

A survey in America showed how, in the ten years since 1956, the value of record sales had gone up from $250 to $650 million. It also showed that there were over 10,500 records released compared to just over 6,100, and single sales were double those of albums, whereas in 1956 it had been 3-1 in favour of singles. Another survey showed how since 1963, records by groups on the chart had increased from 28% to 72%, and records by male soloists had declined from 52% to 20%.

Hollywood also realised there were bucks in the Beat Boom, and constructed their own made-to-measure group, The Monkees. The quartet's TV series *The Monkees*, which owed more than a little to The Beatles' films, bowed on US TV just two weeks after the Fab Four played their last ever American show. Their first single and LP shot to the top of the US chart, and they were one of the 11 American groups who were included in the year's Top 20 singles artists - reducing the number of UK groups to a Beat Boom low of just three. In 1967, The Monkees replaced The Beatles as the world's top selling recording act.

Mods and Minis

SIXTIES STYLE

The youth revolution that had begun with rock'n'roll in the 1950s swung into the 1960s with increasing vigour and by 1963 the style of the decade had begun to emerge. The British people were enjoying an economic boom with no shortage of jobs and fatter pay-packets; there was a growing feeling of freedom and it became an era of optimism and enthusiasm. The increasing opulence of young people meant a rise in their leisure and fashion expenditure. On the fashion front, there were now separate teens'n'twenties styles; clothes had generally become much more casual and were increasingly unconventional. Marketing men were targeting the youth markets like never before - jeans and jackets, hi-fi and holidays, Mini cars and motor-scooters - a whole new section of society had plenty of spare cash to spend.

The ubiquitous Mini shared the roads of the Sixties with legions of scooter-riding Mods

CHANGING ATTITUDES

The Swinging Sixties also became a time of changing attitudes. Ideas and actions which had previously been labelled 'improper' suddenly seemed to become acceptable. The baby boom generation gave birth to the permissive society and their pursuit of pleasure began.

More young people than ever started regularly attending clubs, many of which employed live bands as well as a DJ presenting records. It was British rhythm and blues (along with the age-old reason of meeting the opposite sex in a dimly lit room) that attracted most of these new club goers. R&B venues sprang up all over the British Isles, in back rooms of pubs, in function halls and in cellars, many of which had previously been strongholds of trad jazz. Every city had its 'in' clubs, the best known of them arguably being The Cavern in Liverpool, The Marquee, The Flamingo and The Scene in London's West End, and The Crawdaddy in Richmond. It was at such hot, sweaty, smoke-filled (mostly straight tobacco - though marijuana 'reefers' were not as unknown as some would have us believe) clubs that scores of later rock idols learned their trade. It was also there that the 'faces' learned the effects of the little pills with such names as blues, bennys, dexys, black bombers and of course purple hearts. Cheaply decorated venues like these were where groups like The Rolling Stones, The Who and The Kinks got their start, and where visiting American blues heroes played to wide-eyed (often due to those little pills) British fans.

When thinking of the early 1960s Mods, the picture is of smart Italian-style suits, colourful shirts, chisel toe or cuban heeled shoes and pork pie hats. Within this rough framework, fashions changed fast and furiously, and to be a 'face', it was vital to have the 'right' cut of jacket and trousers ('right' varying too frequently for most teenager's pockets). The 'in' look for shirts also changed almost monthly, with collars going from a short button-down style to a very long pointed look and all stops in between. The man who perhaps did more for mod fashions than anyone else was Glaswegian designer, John Stephen, whose shops in the Carnaby Street

The Beatles' collarless jackets, designed by Pierre Cardin, were soon aped by all and sundry. Below, singer Mark Wynter sports the look in the 1963 pop movie *Just For Fun*

area had been attracting trendy young men since 1957. Mod style even extended to scooters – Vespa and Lambretta were the main manufacturers – the movement's favourite form of transport, which were customised into a show-stopping spectacle with banks of mirrors, lamps and badges.

Beatlemania took Britain by storm in 1963. The Fab Four were groomed by their energetic manager Brian Epstein - the scruffy rockers changed into smart suited 'mop tops'. All they needed (besides love) was their round-necked collarless jackets and elastic-sided ankle boots (originally called Chelsea boots, and then renamed Beatle Boots or Mersey Boots). Their initial outfits were copied by many, and their later fashion items such as John Lennon's peaked cap and the group's military style jacket image were also continually cloned. The Beatles also popularised a 'revolutionary' new hairstyle for young men; longer with a distinctive combed-forward fringe covering the forehead and ears. Generally, men's hair was getting longer, but it was The Beatles who inspired most young men to grow theirs, and to many of the older generation, who were used to 'short back and sides', this more than anything else seemed to spell anarchy!

BOUTIQUE BOOM

The Rolling Stones with their 'no-frills-no-holds-barred' scruffy mod look, complete with shoulder length hair, became a focus for young rebels, many of whom followed groups like The 'Stones and The Who with zeal, copycatting their contempt for upper class values and their experimentation with drugs.

It has to be remembered that during the Beat Boom era a definite North-South battle was going on in Britain, not only in music but also in fashion. Hip Londoners wanted to set the trends and many people outside the capital refused, on principle, to follow their lead. However, most singers of the period did buy their clothes from London shops like those owned by John Stephen. As Liverpool act The Searchers said ' Liverpool is so far behind - London is certainly the best place to obtain fashionable clothes.'

Mary Quant (above) and a model (right) wearing Quant's 'Daddy Long Legs' boots from her Quant Afoot range

"Liverpool is so far behind –

London is certainly the best place to

obtain fashionable clothes"

The Searchers

The success of designer/boutique owners Stephen and Mary Quant spurred on many other young British fashion designers, many of whom also showcased their pop-art outfits and trendy gear in London's 'fab' fashion centres, the Kings Road and Carnaby Street. Mary Quant, doyenne of 1950s fashion (who had opened her first shop, Bazaar, in the Kings Road in 1955 and expanded into wholesale six years later) went from strength to strength with her inventive and uninhibited designs in the early 1960s, and even started exporting to the US in 1963. Another success story was hairdresser Vidal Sassoon, who achieved worldwide fame, firstly with his cleverly shaped 'Bob' and later with other geometric styles. Great Britain began to enjoy an international reputation for its creative young generation and Carnaby Street strutted its stuff and became the symbol of Swinging Britain as well as a top London tourist attraction.

UNION HI-JACK

The sartorial slide of the mid-1960s mods started when they began to swop their smart suits firstly for casual US college-boy styles and then for fur trimmed parkas, Op-Art clothes and T-shirts. The British flag, the Union Jack, which was hi-jacked by the Mods, also became a popular Carnaby Street icon. The Who, in particular, had an Op-Art orientated mod look, featuring the British flag in their clothes; because of their anti-social attitude, the flag came to represent the anti-Establishment stand supported by these new mods. The high points of this era for many mods were the regular Bank Holiday battles with rockers on beaches and in coastal towns up and down the British Isles. The media naturally made a meal of these melees, which inevitably attracted even more mods and rockers to the seaonal seaside scuffles. After all, it was one way (or in most cases the only way) that most of the participants would ever get in the papers or on TV.

By now, many of the older generation were complaining that girls looked like boys (short hairstyles and flat chests) and boys were looking like girls (long hair and flowery shirts)! Unisex clothes, which included the ubiquitous hipster trousers and jeans, were on sale everywhere and the younger generation were happily breaking all the rules about who wore what, when and where.

1965 was the year when the mini dress really took off - and up. Skirts gradually got shorter and shorter till they eventually became 'pelnets'.

142

Long legs were 'cool' and obviously became the focus of attention as women everywhere discovered a new way of walking. Tights replaced stockings and leg-hugging kinky boots were hip. Girls' clothes were being designed with hard, definite edges, often with a hint of the space-age about them, either in the styling or in the use of fabrics like PVC. Much emphasis was placed on contrast; black and white being one of the most popular; and this was echoed in make-up and hair - black, black eyes and pale, pale lips and sleek smooth hard-edged hairstyles. All of this contributed to the famous 'British look', which was exported to the US and the continent.

By this time, discotheques, a concept imported from France, were as much a part of the night life of most cities as the ever-full local Mecca ballrooms. The idea

Mods battle Rockers on the beach at Margate, May 1964. Billie Davis (below) epitomised the short skirt and 'kinky boots' look

The fashion boom hinged on retail outlets such as Biba (right) and the new young models like Jean Shrimpton

of a venue where the clientele danced to records in classy surroundings initially appealed to an older and less hip clientele than the those at a basic R&B club. However, this was soon to change and discotheques also became the 'in places' for most working class teenagers, as a major part of youth culture, they were sung about in songs like Petula Clark's hits 'Downtown' and 'I Know A Place' - the latter having been written at, and about, the 100 Club in London's Oxford Street.

REVOLT IN STYLE

In the mid-1960's, fashion model Twiggy (Lesley Hornby) epitomised the 'little boy' look with her short urchin haircut and adolescent thinness. Measuring only size 6 in dresses, she was a natural for the mini, the tight skinny rib tops, and the undersized styles. Singers such as Lulu donned the more feminine and often frilly little-girl dresses that were part of the 'dolly girl' image, which was successfully presented by models like Jean Shrimpton, Celia Hammond and Patti Boyd. Biba, the boutique, which had been launched by designer Barbara Hulanicki in 1964, summed up all that was adored by the dolly bird. Another more daring fashion for the time was for open knit crochet or see-through tops and dresses but for those who wanted to cover-up, trouser suits became an alternative to the skirt.

Over in the US the first psychedelic fads and fashions had started to filter out of San Francisco during 1965. The city had originally been the heart of the 1950s Beat movement and gradually many born-again-beatniks from all over the US were migrating to the now-legendary Haight-Ashbury area. Folk-rock met acid-rock there and musicians started celebrating with song, sex, drugs and self-expression, but also more seriously, singers were lending support lyrically to the protests of black civil rights movement and the anti-Vietnam draft dodgers.

BEAUTIFUL PEOPLE

By 1966, flower-power was sprouting and the hallucinogenic drug LSD was being used and eulogised. The first psychedelic boutiques-cum-'head shops' opened, selling a freaky mix of flares and ruffles, the embroidered exotic and ethnic, beads and bells and other cheap chic. The innovative San Francisco venue, Fillmore West, masterminded a new experience in clubs with an array of fluorescent-hued flashing lights and multi-coloured moving patterned slides. That summer witnessed the first bloom of flower children 'turning on, tuning in and dropping out' at the San Francisco Trips festival - it was like a test run for the Summer of Love that was to blossom the following year.

The Beat Boom which had started in small, crowded, sweaty, smoke-filled and dark cellar clubs in Britain, had metamorphosed into psychedelic music, and was now being performed in the open air for thousands of 'beautiful people' in California parks – what was known as underground music had persuaded people to come overground.

Twiggy, with her slight figure and big eyes, became the enduring symbol of the Sixties 'dolly bird'

Ready Steady Go-Go

THE BEAT BOOM MEDIA

Hard to believe as it may now seem, Britain had no legitimate all-pop radio station of its own throughout the Beat Boom era. To hear a regular diet of hits, UK listeners had to rely on evening-only broadcasts from the English service of Radio Luxembourg, and (from 1964 onwards) on the illegal pirate radio stations, which broadcast from outside British territorial waters. The Musicians Union still held the BBC in a stranglehold, insisting on restricting 'needle time' (the amount of time actual records could be played on air) so that live musicians could continue to earn money from regular session work.

When 1963 dawned, the best loved pop shows on the BBC's Light Programme were still such early 1960s' favourites as *Parade Of The Pops*, *Go Man Go* and the two shows hosted by Brian Matthew, *Easy Beat* and *Saturday Club*, all of which included a less than ideal combination of records and live performances. Many pop buyers also regularly tuned their 'trannies' (transistor radios, then a new invention) to BBC shows such as *Side By Side*, *Pop-A-Long*, the lunch time show *Let's Go*, *On The Scene* and the classic *Pop Goes The Beatles* series. Among the shows which persuaded listeners to re-tune to Luxembourg on the Fab 208 wavelength were *The Teen & Twenty Disc Club*, *Swoon Club*, *Tony Hall's Top 20*, and regular shows sponsored by such record labels as Decca, Pye and Capitol.

A major contributory factor to the continued success of the British Beat Boom was the introduction of pirate radio. In March 1964, the first pirate ship, Radio Caroline, began broadcasting off the Essex coast, and it was soon claiming as large an audience as Radio Luxembourg. In May 1964, Radio Atlanta started nearby, and before long the two pioneering pirates were joined on the air waves by many more stations including: Radio London (who

Spurred by the success of the pirate broadcasters, in particular Radio Caroline (above), the broadcasting establishment embraced pop as never before; (right) all four Beatles on the panel of top TV show *Juke Box Jury*

JOHN LENNON   PAUL McCARTNEY   RINGO STARR   GEORGE HARRISON

gave a start to John Peel, Kenny Everett and Tony Blackburn), Radio Scotland, Radio Sutch (owned by eccentric performer and would-be MP, Screaming Lord Sutch), Radio 390, Radio City and Radio England (where noted DJ Johnny Walker was first heard). To British ears unaccustomed to American-styled Top 40 radio, these stations were revolutionary. Listeners were impressed by the ear-catching made-in-the-USA jingles aired by the stations and their DJs. They were also surprised that a DJ could carry a show for three or four hours (on the BBC, 30 minutes or an hour was usually tops), and most of the audience even liked to hear the advertisements after decades of the commercial-free BBC. Perhaps the most striking difference between the pirates and the BBC was that pirate DJs sounded, and were, young and keen on the music they played. As run-of-the-mill and boring as all this sounds now, mid-1960s UK pop fans really appreciated and applauded all these innovations.

Disc jockeys had more power in making and breaking hits in the Sixties than any time before or since. Left, top jocks Alan Freeman and Tony Blackburn

MASQUERADE

The BBC did not outwardly try to compete with the Pirates. They stuck with their roster of old-school DJs, many of whom masqueraded as members of the Swinging British scene, despite their obvious ignorance about the music. Under their thin veneer of rock appreciation most clearly preferred cabaret crooners and 'Vegas veterans. During the mid-1960s, while the government was trying to prohibit Pirate pop stations, the government-owned BBC tried to win back listeners with programmes like: *The Joe Loss Show*, hosted by the veteran big band leader, *This Must Be The Place*, *Beat Show*, *Swing Into Summer* and *Saturday Swings*. In addition they also aired the popular *Top Gear*, *Pop Inn* and *Teen Scene*. Finally, in 1967, when the Beat Boom had passed, the BBC heeded the old adage 'if you can't beat them, join them', and launched Radio 1.

Back in 1955, when rock'n'roll was planting its first roots in the United Kingdom, radio ruled the roost and only 4.5 million television licences were issued. Ten years later, when the Beat Boom was at its height, more than 13 million people owned TV sets, and television replaced radio as the most effective and popular medium for promoting music.

The most popular pop TV shows in the UK in 1963 were old favourites, *Thank Your Lucky Stars* and *Juke Box Jury*. Britain's busiest DJ, Brian Matthew, hosted the former show, whose format was simple - pop acts performing their latest singles - while on the latter, a panel of so-called celebrities gave their uninformed opinions on a selection of new singles. Also on the small screen that year were shorter-lived shows such as *Here Comes The Girls* (which not surprisingly featured female pop stars), *Like...Music* ,*The 6.25 Show* (on which The Beatles appeared early in their career) and *Dad You're A Square*, which had a panel of teenagers and their fathers discussing and sometimes literally decimating the latest discs. Artists also popped-up on programmes such as *Scene At 6.30* (which replaced *People & Places*- the show on which The Beatles debuted), Southern TV's *Round Up* and *Tuesday Round Up*. From a musical standpoint, the most important new show of '63 was undoubtedly *Ready Steady Go*, the first TV programme to be aimed directly at the Beat Boom generation. Incidentally, the trend-setting show was first aired in August; a matter of days after *Thank Your Lucky Stars* celebrated its 100th edition.

TOP OF THE POPS

On New Years Day 1964, BBC TV launched *Top Of The Pops*. Jimmy Savile (who like The Beatles was later honoured by the Queen) hosted the first show, and the guests included The Rolling Stones, The Dave Clark Five, The Hollies and Dusty Springfield. Thirty years later the show, whose content was based on the singles chart, is still BBC television's most popular music programme. Also on the box in 1964 were *Top Beat*, which could be seen on the newly established BBC 2 channel, *A Swinging Time* and *The Beat Room*, which The Animals helped to launch. Pop acts also regularly appeared on childrens' programmes such as *Crackerjack* and variety shows like *Sunday Night At The London Palladium*, *Big Night Out* and those hosted by family entertainers Billy Cotton and Arthur Haynes. Celebrated British pop TV producer Jack Good (known for his work on *6.5 Special*, *Oh Boy!*, *Boy Meets Girls* and *Wham!!*), launched his first American TV series, *Shindig*, in September, 1964, and its main rival, *Hullaballoo*, hit US screens four months later. Both programmes proved to be essential tools in helping break British acts on the other side of the Atlantic.

The Beatles (right) on the set of *Ready Steady Go!*, with presenter Keith Fordyce

The 'Stones on *RSG*; manager Andrew Loog Oldham can be seen on the left, behind the camerman, wearing dark glasses

Britain's two top rated pop shows, *Thank Your Lucky Stars* and *Ready, Steady Go*, both needed face-lifts in Spring 1965. The former show abandoned its previously popular 'Spin-A-Disc' spot, where a teenage panel often including Janice 'Oi'll Give It Five' Nichols judged new releases. As part of its new look *TYLS* doubled its studio audience to 700 and allowed half onto the floor (although no dancing was allowed). They also added film clips and interviews to their agenda to win back lost viewers. The spring cleaning of *Ready Steady Go* (which during its existence was hosted by such varied people as mod trend setter Cathy McGowan, and veteran *NME* scribe Keith Fordyce) changed it from a mimed to a live show. Acts like Gerry & The Pacemakers, The Rolling Stones, The Animals and Cliff Bennett were among the first to prove they were not reliant on studio trickery to sound good. In October, with over 200 shows to its credit, *TYLS*, which was still suffering in the ratings battle, reduced the number of acts it featured and changed its emphasis from beat to ballad. By the end of 1965, *RSG* was also having problems and was ear-marked for the television graveyard, although it was reprieved at the eleventh hour when its planned replacements, *It's All Go* and *One Two Three*, failed to excite the TV moguls. Other British shows featuring hit artists in 1965 were hosted by Eamonn Andrews, Kathy Kirby and Dusty Springfield, ABC's variety spectacular, *Blackpool Night Out*, and the pop-packed *Gadzooks It's All Happening, Now* (which replaced *Discs-A-Gogo*) and *Stramash*.

CRAZY WORLD

Some might say that in 1966 Batmania replaced Beatlemania. It was the year that kids (of all ages) went Batman batty on both sides of the Batlantic. It was also the year when British children's telly shows like the puppet-presented *Titch & Quackers*, *Five O'clock Club*, ATV's *Action* and *Hey Presto, It's Rolf* (Harris) regularly featured top recording artists. Among the new pop-slanted shows aimed at a more adult audience in Britain's last monochrome-only TV year were *A Whole Scene Going* hosted by Barry Fantoni and Wendy Varnals, and *The Tom Jones Show*, which was also screened successfully Stateside. Perhaps more importantly, 1966 was the year

when The Monkees' Beatles-inspired TV series was launched in the States (during the same week as *Star Trek*) and *Ready Steady Go*, which more than any other British TV programme represented the Beat Boom age, closed its doors for the last time. Incidentally, early in 1966 *New York Times* ran a story stating 'CBS were close to developing a disc which can reproduce pictures (on your television) as well as sound' adding that 'it could have revolutionary implications in all fields of entertainment.'

While the audience for television was increasing at breakneck speed, attendances at cinemas were decreasing equally rapidly. One reason that many British cinemas were turning into bingo halls may well have been the standard of pop films made in that era.

If proof were needed that few foresaw the Beat Boom, a glance at the casts of 1963s British pop movies would confirm the assertion. One such film was *Just For Fun*, an unlikely tale about the Teenage Party winning the general election, which included Mark Wynter, The Spotnicks, Jet Harris & Tony Meehan and The Tornados, as well as American yesterday-men Freddie Cannon, The Crickets, Johnny Tillotson and Bobby Vee. *Live It Up* was another missed-the-beat-boat movie, which featured Gene Vincent, Heinz (Burt) and Sounds Incorporated. That year also saw the release of *It's All Happening*, and the agreeable musical, *What A Crazy World*. The first of these films included pop has-beens Tommy Steele, Shane Fenton, Russ Conway, Marion Ryan and Carol Deene, while the latter was a vehicle for Joe Brown, Marty Wilde and Susan Maughan; even the last minute addition of zany beat band Freddie & The Dreamers hardly swelled box office receipts.

DON'T LOOK BACK

Among the better British pictures of the era were Cliff Richard's *Summer Holiday*, in which he and The Shadows drove a London bus across Europe, and his *Wonderful Life*, which, although not being world-beaters, were easy-on-the-eye celluloid successes. The highlights of the otherwise below average British pop movie era were without doubt The Beatles' innovative films *A Hard Day's Night* and *Help!*. These not only inspired many other films and TV shows (including *The Monkees*), but also spurred some film critics to compare the group favourably with the Marx Brothers!

The success of these Beatles films triggered off many less-celebrated cinematic moments starring Britain's Beat Boom boys. Gerry & The Pacemakers, Cilla Black and The Fourmost were seen in *Ferry Cross The Mersey*, The Dave Clark Five briefly flirted with film fame in *Catch Us If You Can* (aka *Having A Wild Weekend*) and Herman's Hermits starred in several Hollywood films including *When The Boys Meet The Girls*, *Hold On* and *Mrs. Brown You've Got A Lovely Daughter*. Incidentally, Clark had been a film stunt man before his group took off and Herman (Peter Noone) had been a successful child actor. Madcap Manchester group Freddie & The Dreamers were cast in more movies than most, and many people agree with the American film critic who commented 'All the films they got anywhere near are terrible'. They appeared in such low budget non-starters as *Cuckoo Patrol*, the similarly best forgotten *Out of Sight*, and *Everyday's A Holiday* (known in the US as *Seaside Swingers*). The latter also starred early 1960s UK chart toppers John Leyton and Mike Sarne, and even this author was dragged in as an

What A Crazy World (above) featured Marty Wilde (far left) and Joe Brown (far right)

During the filming of *A Hard Day's Night* Paul McCartney is spotted by one of his more mature fans

extra. However, if one had to select a Worst Film of the Beat Boom Era, it would demand a photo finish, and up there with the leaders would certainly be the pathetically plotted British film, *Gonks Go Beat* (which included an understandably embarrassed Ginger Baker and Graham Bond), and the equally mind-numbing British production, *The Ghost Goes Gear*.

British film makers may have cut corners and underestimated the intelligence of the potential audience for rock-related movies, but they weren't alone. Even though musical movies such as *Mary Poppins*, *The Sound Of Music* and *My Fair Lady* were huge money spinners for them, Hollywood's movie moguls did not invest heavily in the production of less family-orientated musical films. Once Hollywood discovered that America's teenagers were half-fascinated by the California surfing lifestyle, they churned out a seemingly endless wave of inexpensive and poorly scripted beach movies. Among these were: *Bikini Beach*, *Beach Party*, *Muscle Beach Party*, *The Horror of Party Beach* and *Beach Blanket Bingo*. There was also the unforgettable *How To Stuff A Wild Bikini*, *Ghost In The Invisible Bikini* and several dozen other similar cinematic stiffs, most with 'beach' and 'party' related titles. However, it wasn't all sun and fun for America's pop movie makers - they also produced wacky winter teen flicks such as *Wild Wild Winter*, *Ski Party* and *Winter A Go-Go*.

America's most interesting pop films of the period were arguably *Gather No Moss* (known in the US as *The T.A.M.I. Show*), and *Don't Look Back*, a documentary about Bob Dylan's 1965 British tour. The former was simply an all-star live concert starring James Brown, The Rolling Stones, Marvin Gaye, Jan & Dean, The Beach Boys, Chuck Berry and countless others. Odd as it may seem now, the idea of releasing a film of a live show or a rockumentary in those days was considered not only revolutionary, but also financially risky. Although neither picture smashed box office records, they did show the new and exciting direction in which rock movies were heading.

Good Vibrations

SHAPES OF THINGS TO COME

The first of the new breed of 'heavy' blues bands, Cream (above and right) were also the first true supergroup, while Pink Floyd (opposite) pioneered what became known as 'progressive' rock

In those 36 astonishing months since the British Invasion had begun, over 300 singles recorded in the UK had penetrated the American chart. Nevertheless, as the curtain came down on 1966, the number of British hits was decreasing – the last shots of the British Beat Boom were being heard on both sides of the Atlantic. Derek Johnson of *NME* underlined the point by writing: 'British pop is now going through a transitional period. There is a crying need for a new trend, a new sound to revitalise (as The Beatles and Elvis did in the past) an industry which many people think has reached another period of stagnation.' However, all was not

"British pop is now going through a transitional period. There is a crying need for a new trend, a new sound to revitalise (as The Beatles and Elvis did in the past) an industry which many people think has reached another period of stagnation."

Derek Johnson, NME

doom and gloom - the British had learned a lot in a short time about ruling the rock airwaves, and did not intend to call it quits and forget the hits. Their troops were regrouping, re-thinking their strategy and battle plan, and readying themselves for another international aural assault. The Beatles and The Rolling Stones may still have been in the front line, but the vast majority of the backup forces were new, or at least recent, recruits.

FRESH CREAM

Among those who helped point British recording artists in a winning new direction was Jimi Hendrix, an American psychedelic rock singer/guitarist, who had to relocate to the UK to find the world-wide fame his revolutionary style deserved. The Beatles took a block booking at EMI's Abbey Road studio, to start work on their own Pet Sounds equivalent, which they called Sergeant Pepper's Lonely Hearts Club Band. No sooner had they started laying tracks, than news reached them that those Pet Sounds boys, The Beach Boys, had dethroned them in the *NME* Poll as World's Top Group. In December 1966, while many Beat Boom bands acted the fool in pantomime, *Ready Steady Go*, British TV's flagship of the Beat Boom era, put up its shutters for the last time. However, as one door closed, another opened, and on the very next day the BBC announced that in 1967 they would soon be starting their own pop radio station, Radio One; perhaps even more importantly, Fresh Cream, the debut album by blues-rock band Cream, entered the UK chart.

Cream, arguably the first British band predominantley aimed at album buyers, proved to be one of the most important and influential acts of the decade. The ground-breaking blues-based trio spent the vast majority of their short two year life span touring America, the country for which the 'supergroup' concept had been designed, and where their first five albums all went gold. It was the group that thrust Eric Clapton to God-like status, before the intense pressures of fame became more than he and his colleagues, Jack Bruce and Ginger Baker, could tolerate. After Cream played their final concert in November 1968, Clapton and Baker went on to another supergroup, Blind Faith, which folded even more swiftly.

ALBUM ORIENTED

Pink Floyd, who inspired countless artists to climb on the psychedelic bandwagon, opened their chart account with the distinctive hit singles, 'Arnold Layne' and 'See Emily Play' in 1967. They went on to become an all time top album act, with their 1973 release, Dark Side Of The Moon, selling in excess of 12 million copies in America, and staying in the US chart for an unbelievable 13 years! It was a similar story for Cat Stevens (Steven Georgiou), who emerged as a classy pop singer aiming at the singles chart, but after re-inventing himself as a folk-styled singer/songwriter, had a string of top selling transatlantic albums, including the million selling Teaser And The Firecat and the US chart topper Catch Bull At Four. Progressive rock band Traffic, fronted by Steve Winwood (ex-Spencer Davis Group), also started with a 1967 hit single, 'Paper Sun', and later became a very popular LP act. Other album-oriented artists who first came into their own in the late Sixties included Van Morrison and the idiosyncratic Jethro Tull, fronted by the bushy-

> The N'Betweens debuted on Columbia. They later became Ambrose Slade and then Seventies superstars Slade

bearded Ian Anderson, who often played the flute and sang while standing on one leg. Morrison, who had fronted R&B band Them, launched a solo career with a 1967 US Top 10 hit, 'Brown Eyed Girl', before becoming a cult figure among rock fans thanks to a string of classic album releases. Jethro Tull, whose unique mix of folk and progressive rock made them long-standing transatlantic favourites, first made a name for themselves with their debut LP, This Was, in 1968.

PSYCHEDELIC SUPERSTARS

Albums may have achieved an unprecedented importance in the late 1960s, but the pop singles chart was still the main target for most recording artists. Among the more successful new British singles artists breaking through in that era were Engelbert Humperdinck, Mary Hopkin, Amen Corner, Love Affair, Marmalade, The Herd and The Move. The first four groups in the above list were accurately aimed at the ever increasing teeny bop market, while The Move, who among other things destroyed television sets as part of their stage act, were the latest, and one of the most innovative, in a long line of controversy-courting British bands.

Fleetwood Mac, Joe Cocker, Procol Harum, Status Quo, The Bee Gees, Jeff Beck and Humble Pie were among the other artists who first found fame in the final years of the Swinging Sixties. Fleetwood Mac started as a flagship of the new British blues boom, and went on to become one of the world's biggest selling rock album acts. Both Cocker and Procol Harum's chart careers commenced with a No. 1 British single, and both acts went on to sell enviable amounts of albums.

Latter-day hard rockers Status Quo debuted on the singles chart with the psychedelic single, 'Pictures Of Matchstick Men', and re-emerged in the 1970s as Britain's ultimate rock'n'roll boogie band. Although quite different musically, The Bee Gees' fame was equally enduring, and the three brothers' stunning vocal harmonies brought them not only a string of hit singles in the late Sixties, but also the biggest-selling soundtrack album of all time, Saturday Night Fever, ten years later. Ex-Yardbirds guitarist Jeff Beck found himself with two US Top 20 albums in the late 1960s, Truth and Beck-Ola, thanks in no small part to the unique vocal contributions of Rod Stewart. Humble Pie, another so-called 'supergroup', was formed by 'The Face Of 1968', ex-Herd member Peter Frampton, and the equally camera-friendly ex-Small Face, Steve Marriott.

SUMMER OF LOVE

Of course, Britannia didn't rule the rock airwaves exclusively, and American acts were often more popular than their British equivalents. That was especially true of those from California, the state that gave the world Flower Power and which was the epicentre of The Summer Of Love. San Francisco became the trendiest music city in the world in 1967. From its cosmopolitan society came world-beating acid-rock acts like Jefferson Airplane, Grateful Dead, Big Brother & The Holding Company (featuring Janis Joplin, whose immense talent was cut off in its prime in 1970 by a drug overdose), and many others. Down the coast in Los Angeles, things were hotting up too - The Doors, whose first nine albums all went gold and/or platinum, topped the US singles chart with 'Light My Fire', and their charismatic vocalist Jim Morrison's anti-establishment stance made him a hero.

The new faces of the psychedelic era included Procul Harum (above) and the toothsome Brothers Gibb – The Bee Gees

On the East Coast, Andy Warhol's Exploding Plastic Inevitable Revue included a strange group, The Velvet Underground, among whose members were Welsh cello player John Cale, German chanteuse Nico, and a songwriter and vocalist of considerable charisma, Lou Reed. Although they would never be major league record sellers, they influenced countless other acts over the years. Also in New York were early heavy metal exponents Vanilla Fudge and songwriters Neil Diamond and teenager Janis Ian (whose debut hit in 1967 was the controversial 'Society's Child', a song about romance between black and white adolescents).

THE SOULFUL SIXTIES

Before the decade closed, still more world beating bands emerged on both sides of the Atlantic including: Deep Purple, Creedence Clearwater Revival, The Band, Canned Heat and Led Zeppelin. The more down-to-earth sounds of American soul music also gained well-earned popularity around the globe. Leading the soulful surge were Otis Redding (who died in 1967), Aretha Franklin, Wilson Pickett and Sam & Dave, all of whom scored long-deserved international hits in the 'Soulful Sixties'. When the decade finally ended the southern soul capitals of the United

Englebert Humperdinck (above) and The Move were both contenders in the continuing race up the singles charts

First Carter-Lewis and The Southerners, then The Ivy League, by the late Sixties they had become The Flowerpot Men

States, Memphis and Muscle Shoals, had quite justifiably joined Merseyside and Manchester as the musical Meccas of their day.

Late 1960s America also gave the world the first successful rock musical, *Hair*, bubblegum music (the source of many transatlantic pop hits) and rock festivals like Monterey, Altamont and, of course, Woodstock. It was the 'make love not war' era, when both Eastern religions and fashions attracted undreamed of interest from Western teenagers. Words like LSD (which in Britain previously meant pounds, shillings and pence) and tripping took on new meanings, and overnight there was an unbelievable demand for so-called Underground Music. Many musicians ditched their pasts to join the bona fide flower children. These musical chameleons slipped on kaftans, beads and bells and sang of peace and love in the hope that it would help end war forever, or at least bring a little fame and fortune their way. It was a time when 'beautiful people' extolled the delights of love-ins and dropping out, and hordes of recently converted hippies gave the flower trade an unexpected boost. Not only was it a colourful and creative time, but it was also a period when music helped unite the world's youth in a way not witnessed before or since. It was an era of hope, when any changes seemed possible. Unfortunately, the 'love generation' are probably best remembered for making drug-taking fashionable - a trend that still survives today.

The 1960s had seen the pop music business mature beyond belief. Stereo replaced mono, albums became more important than singles for most of the new rock acts, self-contained artists became commonplace, and cover artwork became increasingly more significant as cover versions, thankfully, became less so. The 45 single itself, which had earlier simply signified two minutes of frivolous foot tapping fun, proved it could also be a carrier of important and valid social messages as rock became the vehicle for a generation's conscience. History shows there was far more to the Swinging Sixties than just the Beat Boom, and that two decades later British artists would mount an even more successful invasion on the American charts. Nonetheless, few could deny that 1963-1966 were the most exciting and important years in the history of British pop music.

> **A vocal version of the Highway Code by The Master Singers hit the UK Top 30, closely followed by 'Weather Forecast'**

Index